HOW TO
SEE NATURE

Paul Evans

BATSFORD

For Maria Nunzia

First published in the United Kingdom in 2018 by
Batsford
43 Great Ormond Street
London WC1N 3HZ

An imprint of Pavilion Books Company Ltd.

ISBN: 9781849944939

A CIP catalogue record for this book is available
from the British Library.

10 9 8 7 6 5 4 3 2 1

Reproduction by Rival Colour Ltd, UK
Printed and bound by Toppan Leefung Printing Ltd, China

This book can be ordered direct from the publisher
at the website:
www.pavilionbooks.com, or try your local bookshop.

Contents

Introduction

CLOUD COVER HIDES GYRN GOCH ('red horns' in Welsh), a mountain on the northern edge of the Llyn Peninsula in North Wales, and drizzles on the roof of our van that is parked below a tumble of cottages with the same name as the mountain and on the rabbits nibbling the campsite grass. We walk down to the shingle edging an incoming tide. A small brook passes between the grey, cloudy mountain and the grey, cloudy sea, under cliffs called Aberavon, about 9m (30ft) high. These cliffs are the remains of a raised beach formed at the end of the last Ice Age by sand and shingle dumped from a retreating ice cap when the sea level was much higher. The sand cliffs have been bitten into by storms and the piles of debris on the beach and hanging fence posts above bear witness to recent erosion. Along the cliffs are a scattering of holes, mostly the size made by the circle of thumb and forefinger of two hands together, but some are larger and in shapes that suggest keyholes, letterboxes, slots and squares. I am reminded of an archaeology article describing mysterious holes drilled into cliffs of the River Nile in Sudan, which were discovered to have supported shelters made by people in the Mesolithic period, some 10,000 years ago. The deliberately excavated holes in the Aberavon cliffs may have changed as a result of erosion, but they too have been here for many thousands of years. Suddenly, as if from nowhere, their mining inhabitants come flying home low over the waves and we find ourselves as spectators inside a returning hunting party, a flock or 'richness' of sand martins.

Surprised, enchanted and delighted to be surrounded by wild birds going about their own business, and mindful not to interfere or frighten them away, we retreat to a distance where our presence seems not to affect the sand martins that have come back to feed their chicks in the cliff-hole nests. From this vantage point, my wife, Maria, takes photographs and I stand watching the birds, cliffs, sea. I am looking but how do I see these birds and how do I see Nature in general? Having been asked to write this book, this question has become a challenge. *How to See Nature,* written by the naturalist Frances Pitt (1888–1964), was first published by Batsford in 1940 and it's a privilege for me to look over her shoulder 70 years later. Through an odd serendipity, it turns out we both come from Shropshire and she lived just along the road from where I live now. When I was a child I loved her photographs for Brook Bond Tea Cards and I used to go to Ludlow Museum specially to see the insect collection she donated. She wrote books about the rescued badgers, otters and squirrels she kept as pets, as well as works on British wild animals and plants made from close observation and dedicated study for a lay audience. *The Spectator* criticised her natural-history writing for its interruptions by anecdote and digression, something I too am guilty of. In other respects, we are worlds apart. Frances Pitt was a master of fox hounds and vice-president of the British Field Sports Society; her conservatism had its roots in a near-feudal countryside. *How to See Nature* was written during the upheavals of the Second World War, for evacuees who found themselves far from the city, finding sanctuary from the Blitz and yet cast into the alien environment and culture of the British countryside that many families had lost direct ties with generations ago. Reading her today, Pitt sounds haughtily patronising, but I think she felt a personal responsibility to educate for integration, not only to equip the evacuees with a respect for the wild animals and plants of the countryside that she loved, but also its traditions and values – for her the two were inextricably linked. Her pursuit of natural history was in parts recreational and educational: a lived experience through which she described 'our' countryside ordered into road and lane, field and wood, river and stream, common and heath, pond, marsh and moor; and a useful guide for visitors to the countryside inspired by a growing enthusiasm for wildlife. In this way the book formed a bridge to the wider natural-history literature.

How *I* see Nature in the environmentally anxious early 21st century differs radically from Frances Pitt; I have a very different background, views and access to information; the countryside has changed; so has Nature, so have the people who see it. As I watch the sand martins, these ancient nomads living in an environment as unstable and ever-changing as the sands of the shore, I feel an immense privilege that I can witness their presence and know something about their lives. The sand martins (*Riparia riparia*) are brownish members of the swallow tribe, they look like house martins, only slightly out of focus. They cross the Sahara from Senegal or Mali to come to Britain each spring to breed here. The females excavate or restore their community nest holes in riverbanks, lakesides and sea cliffs, which must be like tunnelling with a pencil. The males join them and help to create a chamber carpeted with feathers, pieces of grass and inevitable parasites, at the end of a 1m (3¼ft) tunnel for the four or five eggs that are laid. The birds feed their brood on insects caught in flight or else plucked from the strandline. They get their riparian name from inhabiting the water's edge: a place where the river, lake or sea has deposited material solid enough to burrow into, where it has shaped it into banks and cliffs high enough to be beyond the reach of predators, and next to open water, vegetation and debris for hunting. This riparian edge is in a constant state of flux from wind, rain, storm, flood, waves and human activity – there are many places where sand martin colonies have been constructed in artificial berms or concrete to compensate for those lost to sand extraction. As the cloud lifts from Gyrn Goch, the sand martins seem caffeinated by the bright June sunlight. They pass low over the sea with more flutter and less swoop than house martins and swallows; their rasping, gritty contact calls sound urgent and they suddenly form a circle of around 30 adults and juveniles, clamouring around the cliff's nest holes, dancing in the air like gnats, while a couple of pairs feed peeping chicks yet to fledge. The birds split up, fly off, come back in ones and twos, in groups of a dozen, full of restless energy – the embodiment of their collective noun. They will leave in October to return to Africa and wintering-ground dramas. Their cliff nests will become temporary roosts for strangers also heading south. Like the people who scraped graffiti into the crumbling Aberavon cliffs – hearts, dates and names – the sand martins have carved their identity into the walls of their ancient unsettled settlement and with it a story of a culture thriving on flux.

I don't know how much sand-martin life has changed in 10,000 years of migration between West Africa and Britain, or how much each journey of 10,000 miles (16,000km) transforms the individual bird; perhaps we, the inconstant ones, will learn nothing from them. But perhaps they unspool for us a thread of wonder in these otherwise mean-spirited times. During this environmental, social and political turbulence, *How to See Nature* is written for an audience sophisticated by 70 years of natural history broadcasting on radio and television: an audience anxious about climate change, habitat destruction and species extinctions, turning to Nature for sanctuary, solace, wellbeing and inspiration;

perhaps looking back with nostalgia to a version of a world
described by Frances Pitt and her contemporaries, such
as Henry Williamson and Gavin Maxwell; perhaps turning
forwards with a contemporary reshaping of what nature writing
might become.

Like the original, this book also wanders, on nature walks
of happenstance, a creative hunter-gathering that starts with an
encounter of wild things and searches for an ecological literacy,
woven from sciences and arts, which attempts to understand
and articulate their 'thingness', as the poet Colin Simms
says. Similarly, Maria's images are drawn, quite literally, from
imprints of memory and experience of things encountered
on our wanderings together. This is a kind of psychoecology
for a multicultural audience that may or may not have
roots in this countryside, but find themselves in a matrix of
brownfield edgelands, transport corridors, urban greenspace,
industrialised agriculture, suburban expansion, rural
development, fragments of ancient countryside and protected
landscapes – places that are nevertheless full of Nature to see.

As I finished the previous sentence I received a call from
the optician reminding me that I'm late for an eye-test
appointment. I return to this paragraph in the knowledge
that I have forming cataracts and this brings home to me how
fragile the ability to see really is. Seeing is believing? Nature –
however we see it and whatever it means to us – is existence,
it is what our consciousness is conscious of. How we see is
very much influenced by our values and attitudes, moods and
emotions, beliefs and curiosity, and that influences how Nature
is represented. However, what we see can also change us: often
it is the common things we overlook that exert such fascination
and wonder when we encounter them and through them we
see the world differently. *How to See Nature* has a sense of
urgency because hard-won advances in nature conservation

and environmental protection can and are being easily reversed and the Anthropocene – which in itself shows the growing acknowledgement that the human action behind climate change, mass extinction and global environmental turmoil is as defining of this era as geological processes were of the past – has changed how we represent what Nature is.

Despite those anxieties, this is still natural history, still writing about wild lives, animals and plants, where they are, what they do, what we know about their lives and interactions with place, each other and ourselves. Nature shows us that the existence of things is shaped by the relationships between them. However, Western culture is conflicted about Nature. On one hand, we are aware of our biophilia, described by the evolutionary biologist E.O. Wilson as the urge to affiliate with other forms of life, a love of Nature embedded in our DNA. On the other hand, we suffer from ecophobia – the fear of Nature's answering the consequences of our existence on Earth with violent retribution, from which we have tried to protect ourselves and now realise our retaliation has gone too far.

I intend the perspective of this book to be one of advocacy for what we see – bringing overlooked wildlife into focus as a way of revealing how it matters. Much of the contemporary discussion about how Nature matters has focused on ideas of natural capital and ecosystems services, and although the importance of Nature to human survival and wellbeing is undeniable, seeing Nature as a resource to be exploited and commodified is a denial of its intrinsic value. The kinds of caring we have for Nature – standing up for it through celebration and advocacy and standing in for it through conservation and management – is a cultural project and the natural history I write (my take on nature writing) and Maria's illustrative drawings form a contemporary narrative, a synthesis of art, science, history, folklore and personal experience.

Throughout my life as a gardener, conservationist, writer, broadcaster and academic, I have been inspired by many people and their works have taught me much; my apologies to those I do not properly acknowledge for their support and guidance; at least my mistakes, I am happy to say, are of my own making. Watching the sand martins' dancing flight around the caring of their young and listening to the communal chatter that articulates their richness, I realise that although we may never understand each other, this writing and drawing is not so much about them as for them.

<u>1</u> The Garden of Delights

Little fly
Thy summer's play,
My thoughtless hand
Has brushed away.

Am not I
A fly like thee?
Or art not thou
A man like me?

For I dance
And drink and sing;
Till some blind hand
Shall brush my wing.

If thought is life
And strength and breath,
And the want
Of thought is death,

Then am I
A happy fly,
If I live,
Or if I die.

WILLIAM BLAKE, 'The Fly'

A MORNING IN JULY, pegging out washing on the line in my garden and a small fly hovers between me and a pair of underpants. The definition of 'to hover', the dictionary says, is 'to remain aloft, suspended and also to be undecided, to linger solicitously'; a hoverfly is a wasp-like fly that hovers and darts. The hoverfly, 10mm (⅜in) long, its wings a blur, maintains a constant position in the air, deciding; its earnestness suggests questioning. It is small enough to defy gravity, creating a cushion of air for buoyancy while it inspects the pants, recognises colour, senses temperature, humidity, chemical transmission and structure, dabs its pad-like mouthpiece on the fabric and sips, and while it processes all this data the fly allows the sun to flash on the amber bands of its body. Then it is gone.

The fly is *Episyrphus balteatus*, nicknamed the marmalade hoverfly, because of the striking orange-peel bands on its abdomen. It is one of the most ubiquitous of the Syrphidae flies – true flies because they have a single pair of wings, unlike bees, butterflies and beetles that have two – and commonly called hoverflies because of their ability to stay motionless in the air. Male marmalade hoverflies are territorial and can hover up to 5m (16½ft) above the ground in a shaft of sunlight to attract females and fend off rivals. The adults feed on nectar and they are one of the few flies to be able to break pollen grains to eat them; they are particularly attracted to yellow or white flowers. Hoverflies are anthropophilic – human-loving – in their choice of dwellings, but the more accurate term for such fellow travellers that make a living in the intimate spaces we create around ourselves, is synanthropic. They are close to us.

'Close,' is not just a description of proximity, it is also the name of a courtyard, quadrangle, an enclosure within the architecture of a religious or civic building, and the origin of what the Elizabethans called the 'garden of delights'. Although cultivating plants for culinary, medicinal, cosmetic and fragrance purposes had been central to human dwelling for centuries, the growing of flowers for pleasure and display in intimate spaces of beauty and contemplation became a phenomenon of medieval cathedrals, monasteries, universities and great houses, and was much imitated. Because of this rather aspirational esoteric idea, 'close' is often the name given to a cul-de-sac – a suburban house-and-garden idyll. I once lived in a close that was a small cluster of houses with open-plan front gardens built in the 1960s on the footprint of a derelict 18th-century priory – inhabited for a few months in 1809 by the curate Patrick Brontë, long before he was the father of famous daughters – and now called Priory Close. When John Clare wandered the English countryside in 1825 admiring, 'flat spreading fields checkerd with closes,' he was describing bright flowering weeds, such as charlock, poppy and cornflower, growing wild but in garden-like patches within the grain crop and, 'troubling the cornfields with destroying beauty'. This pastoral vision was alien to our 20th century close; its garden plants may not have held the same religious, folkloric or cultural symbolism as they did for the previous inhabitants and their medieval predecessors; the weeds that troubled their cultivation may not have been described as 'destroying beauty', but the tensions between what was a garden plant and what was a weed were still very warlike.

Under my current washing line, flower the flat, white, carrot family umbels of ground elder, *Aegopodium podagraria*. Tradition dictates that ground elder is a Eurasian plant that came to Britain with the Romans. That makes it an archaeophyte, a plant introduced and naturalised here before the 15th century, as were the arable weeds brought by Neolithic farmers thousands of years before John Clare admired them.

It is the nature of colonialism and imperialism that occupying cultures bring their synanthropic plants and animals with them, deliberately or by accident. The British certainly have done this with tragic effects throughout the world, introducing plants and animals that have completely changed whole ecosystems. The 17th-century herbalist Nicholas Culpeper included the name 'Æthiopian Cumin-seed' in his *Complete Herbal*, but mainly referred to ground elder as bishop weed: perhaps a satirical common name derived from its use in treating gout, a condition thought to be the result of over-indulgence, or maybe its pestilential reputation as a weed. Culpeper described bishop weed as owned by Venus because it, 'provokes lust to purpose'; this feels particularly true for the insects visiting the Shakespearean theatre of enchantments of what we now call ground elder flowers.

There's something Elizabethan about the ashy mining bees that arrive on these flowers. The females are 10mm (⅜in) long, black with a bluish reflection, a ruff of grey hair, a further grey ring around the thorax and a furry white facial mask. The males are smaller, squatter and less strikingly marked. *Andrena cineraria* is one of 67 species of mining bee in Britain and Ireland. These are hairy little sprites with pollen baskets on their back legs, short tongues and pointed antennae, and are the most effective of pollinators. They excavate nests underground in all kinds of soils. Sometimes they nest in aggregations that can number thousands, although *Andrena* bees are thought of as solitary rather than social insects. Even though there is no evidence of cooperative worker behaviour, they do appear to be moving together, but more like a dance than a factory. The marmalade hoverflies are individuals, feeding on the lush ground elder and setting their sexual vibrations loose from hovering wings in the surrounding air. Once mated, the females lay white, baroquely sculptural eggs in foliage close to an aphid colony. The hoverfly larva are translucent grubs with a respiratory tube at the back end and mouth hooks at the front with which they pierce their aphid prey and suck out their body contents. A larva may eat 200 aphids in its month-long lifecycle, which is why they're used as biological pest control in crops. They are also cannibals.

The marmalade hoverfly is Palaearctic and found across Europe, North Africa and North Asia from Britain to Japan, but strangely for such a capable traveller, the species has not found its way to the New World. The British population is often increased by migration. In particularly good hoverfly breeding conditions there can be such a build-up of the population in continental Europe that, with fine weather and a light southerly breeze, huge numbers will begin a northerly migration. Migrations recorded from the Balearic Islands and Sardinia show the hoverfly's ability to cross the Mediterranean from North Africa. I remember being astonished when I was told the tiny, fragile creature levitating like a cluster of pixels in my backyard may have flown there from the gardens of Marrakesh. However, public empathy with individual lives can be discounted when they become innumerable. Swarms of these wasp-like flies arriving on the British coast, like those in 2004, cause panic headlines and the language of fear and disgust towards such a mass is strikingly similar to that applied to mass migrations of people. The synathropic nature of hoverflies also leads to their destruction: pesticides that kill aphids kill hoverflies. In the kind of irony on which the Anthropocene is built, the eradication of aphids infesting garden plants – an essential prey species for many animals – also eradicates the hoverfly, which is not only an aphid predator but also one of the most prolific pollinators.

A summer generation of marmalade hoverflies may migrate south in the autumn. Many of those that remain, including some larvae, will try to hibernate in ivy or sheds or rot holes in trees. On sunny winter days, they may emerge to warm themselves and dance in sunbeams. There is in hoverflies something of the medieval imagination: creatures hovering over a threshold between the almost supernatural and natural history. Their dangerous wasp disguise conceals sprites employed in the magical work of pollination. Their collective hover-dart-hover behaviour is like the movements of neurons in a Pan-like brain; they exhibit a will and purpose that suggests thought; they question our assumptions. This may be a lot to read into a fly sniffing underpants on a washing line, but isn't it precisely this vernacular, intimate encounter that creates a sense of community with all life?

Of all the communities we and wildlife find ourselves members of, the garden is one of the most intimate. For many, gardens are defined by ownership, territorial rights and the responsibility for its cultivation, which may be a pleasure, an anxiety or a mixture of both. For others, a garden and its 'close' contact with Nature, repose, sanctuary and enclosure may be defined by public access, even if that access is limited by abilities. Gardening is the performance of the movement of Nature into culture. That particular performance is the link between cultivation and civilisation. The result is neither entirely natural nor entirely cultural but a chimera of the two. Human intervention, the kind of care that stands in for natural processes through cultivation, is most directly seen in the design, construction, planting and maintenance of gardens, but it is also present in the historical management of grassland, woodland, heathland and moorland, and more recently in nature conservation management. Benign neglect, the kind of care that stands up for Nature through advocacy and protection, is never truly devoid of human values and preferences, and certainly inseparable from climate change, pollution, habitat destruction and species extinctions. Even in the most manicured gardens, those without ground elder for example, there are synanthropic species that are desired – gardeners' friends such as robins, bumblebees, hedgehogs and song thrushes – and those which are detested – pests such as slugs, rats, wasps and greenfly. The ecological relationships between these two groups of species may be indifferent to human interests but they will, of course, be directly or indirectly affected by them. Privilege may not afford any degree of protection: the tragic decline of the much-loved hedgehog, and the rapid decline of bees, butterflies, frogs and songbirds, are obvious examples. These favoured species have become collateral damage in a war against garden slugs, aphids, ants, wasps, fungi, moss and the weeds Richard Mabey describes as, 'plants that find themselves in the wrong culture'; an onslaught that may hardly trouble the populations of the intended victims of such persecution.

All this division into the favoured and the despised appears in startlingly brilliant visual form in the famous triptych by Hieronymus Bosch, painted c.1480–1505, that came to be called *The Garden of Earthly Delights*. Having been evicted from the original Garden of Eden, the descendants of Adam and Eve in Bosch's strange garden ecology find themselves in a psychedelic drama of creation that is producing hybrids between people, other animals and plants, and damnation, which is recycling them. The painting's viewer becomes voyeur, observing Nature, complicit in the pursuit of pleasure through eroticism and torture, in a dream of intoxicating delirium but nevertheless, an ecological garden vision.

In another garden of delights, the head of a decapitated pigeon began to separate further from its body like some ghastly Victorian séance, or at least that is how it looked. A few windfalls lay under the apple tree and I watched them being gnawed by wasps and delicately tapped by peacock butterfly proboscises in the September sunshine. A small clatter of jackdaws settled in the oak tree and a robin sang from the damson. Mist had cleared and that light, which was on the threshold between late summer and autumn, warmed the colours of the garden. My eye was drawn to a bundle of feathers on the lawn, wings folded neatly to its sides, on its back, grey and still: a pigeon. The head was missing; there was just a bloody stump on its neck and no sign of other injuries. This did not look like the work of a peregrine or sparrowhawk – there were no plucked feathers around the body and no opened chest cavity. This looked like the work of a cat, a kill for killing's sake – an art. However, it didn't account for the missing head, perhaps eaten, perhaps taken as a trophy. With only a greenwood lyric from the robin, the air was still and warm and soft. The day had a gentleness to it until, returning to the dead pigeon, the head had reappeared. Oddly big, round and brown, it was moving away from the body, and then back onto its neck. I darted around the oak tree to see what was going on – the head was in fact a hedgehog. It was chewing on the pigeon's neck, backing off, turning around as if in delight, and returning to continue its meal.

Hedgehogs have not been common here for years now and are extinct in many gardens. Despite there being plenty of good hedgehog habitats throughout the UK, half the rural population and one-third of the urban population has disappeared this century. Hedgehogs are generalists, they forage for beetles, caterpillars and earthworms, and relish opportunities for birds' eggs and carrion. Historically nocturnal creatures of woodland edges, copses, pasture and of course the hedges that act as refuge and connecting byways between them, hedgehogs adapted well to manmade habitats, such as gardens, parks and urban greenspace. Hedgehogs travel surprising distances and require an area of 25–124 acres (10-50ha) to sustain them, regularly walking over 1km (⅔ mile) for a night's foraging. From November to March, they need safe, warm, dry places to lay up inactively. Their major problems are barriers: roads with heavy traffic, walls and hard fences, paved gardens. Once these barriers fragment hedgehog foraging grounds, the population does not have enough space to sustain itself, individuals can't breed, and they become vulnerable to predation and being killed by cars or garden machinery. Every year in Britain, hedgehogs are among the five million wild animals injured as a result of their encounters with people. As wildlife and people become increasingly close, the consequences of our actions become more acute.

Gardens account for about one-quarter of the land area in Britain's towns and cities, and so are important for offsetting some of the effects of climate change through plants absorbing CO_2, cooling urban microclimates and supporting wildlife, and for soil absorbing rainwater run-off and reducing flooding. However, urban areas only make up 7–8 per cent of the country, and only about one-quarter of that is garden, and so the impact of gardeners on wildlife is very small compared to that of farmers. The real importance of gardens is that they hold wildlife where people are. Recent studies show that ordinary gardens, where gardeners do everyday gardening things, are great for wildlife.

The marmalade hoverfly, the ashy mining bee and all the other tiny flies are synanthropic members of that community we may think of as the garden of delights, where the strangeness of Nature is far more bizarre than anything dreamt of by Hieronymus Bosch; it's just a matter of scale. In the poem that opened this chapter, William Blake, with characteristic ecological vision, understood the bond between the almost supernatural actors in the drama of the close.

2 Gardens of Light

A STREETLIGHT IN THE LANE enamelled hollies with
a sodium glow and sucked the colour from the leaves of other
trees, the church bell rang eight or perhaps nine, there was
a soughing through the limes. It was late October, almost
Halloween. 'Night comes:' wrote Nietzsche, 'O, that I have to
be light! That I must thirst for things of night! For solitude!'
Suddenly I felt a tiny sonic boom and the draught of a bat's
wing so close to my ear. It was like a tap on the shoulder, not
a shock so much as a greeting, but all the same I was jolted
from thoughts about one world into another where solitude
is only my failure to see the night filled with unseen lives that
collide with mine.

I took the bat wings to belong to a pipistrelle, *Pipistrellus
pipistrellus:* matchbox-sized ginger bats with wings of black
latex and little bulldog grins. Incidentally, I'm told that if a
bat shows its teeth, you are having an ultrasound scan; its
voice, unheard by you, is establishing your identity. Pipistrelles
are the most common species hereabouts; they hunt the lanes,
fields and park nearby and roost in many roofs including mine,
but unlike them I don't have a built-in ultrasound imager to
identify them accurately. The bats' flight cut through the pool
of lamplight from surprising directions; they were making
elliptical orbits that seemed erratic when all I could see was
their strikes at flies and moths attracted to the fatal beauty of
the illumination.

I knew from recordings of bat detectors that if I could tune into the frequency of the pipistrelle's ultrasound ecolocation I would enter an aural nightscape of digital percussive frenzy, like the electronic equivalent of baying hounds, as the bats hunted, detecting and snapping up as many insects from the air as they could to bulk up for winter – 3,000 a night each is one estimate. Apart from some pipsqueaking and the whirr of wings, I heard nothing. The smaller insectivorous bats, Microchiroptera, evolved echolocation, also called biosonar – their system of ultrasonic signalling using sounds emitted through their mouths and noses reflected back by things in the landscape so rapidly they can detect if an object is hard or soft, stationary or moving, and at what speed and direction it is travelling in. D.H. Lawrence, watching Florentine bats with a growing chill of revulsion wrote:

Pipistrello!
Black piper on some infinitesimal pipe.
Little lumps that fly in air and have voices indefinite,
wildly vindictive.

Despite some lingering prejudices about bats, based on anxieties such as hair entanglement (a superstition), vampirism (restricted to Central and South America) and rabies (not recorded in British pipistrelles), general attitudes towards them have changed dramatically through an increasing understanding of the near magic of echolocation – a superpower they share with whales and dolphins as well as shrews – their uniquely endearing appearance and their vulnerability to human doings. Due to farming practices that have caused the loss of three-quarters of flying insects in recent decades, climate change, disturbance and destruction of roost sites and toxic timber treatment in buildings, the pipistrelle population crashed in the late 20th century. All 17 British breeding bat species and their roosts now have legal protection; the overall population, although still in trouble, has in general terms risen since the year 2000.

In the 18th century, the Jesuit professor of natural history in Pisa, Lazzaro Spallanzani, cut out the eyes of bats and was astonished that they could fly and navigate without them, and believed bats must have a sixth sense. I once had a laboratory specimen of a pipistrelle bat: wings open as if crucified, immersed in a glass box of formalin to preserve it; removed from its elemental darkness and displayed like that, the little bat retained an unsettling uncanniness, as if its sixth sense was still communing with a nocturnal realm beyond its box. Research continues but it is not yet possible to know what bats hear and how they discriminate. However, it is possible to imagine ultrasound images similar to those used medically to see into our bodies, not as detailed as visual images – they have good eyesight for that – but defocused due to the comparatively long wavelengths of sound frequencies. At 45kHz with a wavelength of 7mm (¼in), pipistrelle echolocation is the 'infinitesimal pipe' on which that particular species pipes its own characteristic frequency. Bats whistle in radar on FM (frequency modulation) frequencies: a broadband signal that sweeps down through the sonic range to provide time measurements of distances with an accuracy in tenths of a centimetre, a trick they evolved 54 million years before humans 'invented' radar. They can then switch from FM to CF (constant frequency) frequencies, a narrowband signal that remains constant, producing a characteristic 'hockey-stick' image on a spectrograph, and assess the precise distance and speed measurement of the object they are tracking, alternating from FM to CF at close range. Whether this sounds 'wildly vindictive', as D.H. Lawrence noted, depends on one's point of view.

The energy for flight and the fat reserves needed for hibernation – or at least a fitful sleep with forays in warm spells – requires a mass nightly slaughter of moths, flies, lacewings and beetles. This kind of feeding is not a simple matter of trawling through the night air to scoop up any amount of unidentified flying insects. Bats hunt by detection and pursuit; they locate, identify and chase the insect, reaching out with a wingtip or tail membrane to pull it into their mouths. These manoeuvres can be repeated every few seconds and require a precision and agility of astonishing complexity. However, one of the reasons bats have evolved such skills is because their prey has evolved skills to avoid capture. Moths from the family Noctuidae, such as large yellow underwing, heart and dart, and autumnal rustic, have 'ears' in the form of tympanal organs either side of their thorax that are sensitive to bat ultrasound frequencies. They may consist only of a couple of nerve cells each, but because the moths have no other use for sound, these ears are tuned in specifically to the bat threat. When the moth is stimulated by weak ultrasound, the bat is distant, so the moth flies away. If the signal is strong, the bat is approaching, so the moth begins looping in unpredictable patterns or closes its wings for a free-fall drop to the ground. The bright colours of tiger moths warn predators of their toxicity but because that doesn't work at night with bats, they have developed aposematism – an acoustic signal to advertise their unpalatability – and some have even created a biosonar jamming system. Tiger beetles produce ultrasonic snaps as a deterrent when detecting bat frequencies; dung beetles drop to the ground and walking beetles freeze; crickets – which also communicate in ultrasound – change direction when dispersing or migrating; some flies can 'hear' and react to bats and lacewings have 'ears' in their diaphanous wings that function as bat detectors. All this drama takes place beyond my ability to see and hear it and is happening on a parallel plane of existence.

For a long time, out of sight meant out of mind and because we were quite literally in the dark, nocturnal life was regarded as transgressive, alien or quasi-supernatural; day represented life, reality and good; night represented death, magic and evil. Now, with the aid of sonic detectors, infrared and thermal imagers, we have a glimpse into this dark world that almost touches us. The pipistrelles, although weighing no more than a 20 pence piece, are more closely related to us than they are to mice, and yet, according to Thomas Nagel in his essay, 'What is it Like to be a Bat?' (Nagel, 1974), their perception of the world through echolocation is so alien that we cannot know what it is 'like.'

Imagining ourselves being a bat is not the same as a bat being a bat; we're just not mentally equipped. However, this should not lead us to believe bats have emotional experiences any less rich than our own. Nagel described the bat's ultrasound emission as a 'shriek,' a suitably gothic representation similar to D.H. Lawrence's 'wildly vindictive' voice. More recent research reveals that when bat recordings are slowed down they sound like birdsong; slowed down further they sound like whales and dolphins. Echolocating bats are now thought to be able to eavesdrop on other bats, listening in to identify individuals or foraging groups. They can focus on their own navigation while picking up signals from other bats at a slightly different frequency. Neural mechanisms in bats show they can tune into their own frequency to prevent their signal from being jammed by other bats – and perhaps the distracting white noise of flying insects – in close proximity. Neuroscientists think they process two types of brain signals from opposite halves of the brain. While either the right or left sides of the cerebrum processes echolocation signals, the left side can be processing communicative signals and the echolocation of others. However inadequate our perception of batness, we share with them a manic curiosity, an insatiable appetite and a desperate need to adapt and evolve to circumstances that are adapting against us. Facts can alter the imagination and neuroscience is helping us to see connections between living beings that can be represented in new ways.

Momentarily, under the streetlight, the shimmering pixels of insect wings can be seen as flashing dots of synapses and neurons, like the speeding lights of traffic in the darkness; a network of impulses regulating insect behaviour reacting to the traffic of those synapses and neurons flashing through the mammalian brain of the bat regulating its behaviour towards them and, of course, the same neurological impulses coursing through me, the observer, producing echoes to bat voices I cannot hear. This representation works as a metaphor, with images familiar to a technological culture, but it doesn't bring with it the long history of the uncanny, emotionally edgy feelings embedded in my nocturnal experience. I relish these feelings of strangeness and mystery, and do not dismiss them as arcane relics of superstition; I still 'thirst for things of night', as Nietzsche put it. What brings together all these experiences and interactions with ecological and psychological processes, the intersection around which all this gyrates, is the orange glow of the light.

These pipistrelles, looping from the dark around the streetlamp may not be directly attracted to light, but the insects they hunt are. Unlike species such as greater horseshoe bats which are light averse, pips are the most common bat species in urban areas and are becoming more reliant on towns for buildings to roost in and parks and gardens to hunt in. Bats generally require connecting patches of darkness and are vulnerable to artificial lighting in housing, industrial development, and infrastructure such as streets, roads and motorways that disrupt their flight lines along the commuter routes – the dark corridors of tall hedges and woodland edges they take from roost to hunting ground. This crash-barrier effect forces them to travel further for food. Bat roosts are vulnerable to artificial light and since most flying insects are most active just after sunset, any delay from light disorientation to bats leaving the roosts is a loss of precious feeding time. Artificial light disrupts the normal 24-hour pattern of light and dark and the circadian rhythms of animals and plants that have evolved over millions of years. It disturbs insect feeding and breeding activity, reducing and fragmenting insect populations. It has been estimated that one-third of flying insects die as a result of their encounter with artificial light; the light confuses and exhausts them and makes them vulnerable to predation. It also diverts pollinators from flowers. Research in Switzerland revealed there were less than half the number of visits by night-pollinating insects and fewer species of those insects under artificial lights. Night pollinators such as moths are more efficient than day pollinators at spreading pollen. Lights drawing pollinating insects take them away from pollinating flowers, leading to fewer plants and therefore fewer daytime pollinators, too. The effect on moth communities and other nocturnal insects shows a long-term decline. Artificial light also disrupts circadian rhythms in flowering plants, altering scent emission and nectar production, and thus unravelling relationships between night and day pollinators. Moths, craneflies, midges and lacewings, are particularly attracted to lights with a UV (ultraviolet) component, blue or green lights, and those with short wavelengths and high frequencies. Male moths are particularly drawn to UV light and won't feed or mate in it. The hypothesis about the fatal attraction of moths to the flame or any artificial light is that moths evolved a navigation technique based on celestial bodies called transverse orientation. The moth flies in a straight line by detecting the Moon, fixing its direction by maintaining a constant angle of flight towards its focus, which is so far away that even at great distances the angle is constant. The Moon remains in the upper part of the moth's visual field or on the horizon. A closer light changes the angle in short distances, often below the horizon, so the moth attempts to correct its angle by turning towards the light and so spirals closer to the light source. Pipistrelles will swarm around the Moon-like white mercury (metal halide) lights to hunt dazzled insects but the rarest bats are now those that are averse to artificial light; their worlds are shrinking into puddles of draining darkness. A proliferation of artificial lights increases the opportunity for bat predation by birds, which is the reason they evolved as nocturnal fliers. There are reports of kestrels hunting bats around motorway lights. Perhaps this is a triumph of civilisation: a 24-hour culture, a safer society, shining the light of reason, illuminating the past's darkness. Bats and moths are collateral damage in the war against Nature, a delayed consequence of the struggle to purge the ignorance and superstition those creatures of the night came to represent. Now there have been great advances in bat conservation; they are seen as cute, and suitable for our sanitised version of Halloween.

Artificial lights have a profound effect on the ecology of the world around us. The more they proliferate the greater the effect. Safety – the reduction of traffic accidents and crime – is the justification for the human colonisation of night, but the global spread of artificial lighting is responsible for a pollution that is visible from space but obscures space from Earth; most Europeans now live under skies that are above the threshold for light pollution and all of us live with the pollution caused by keeping the lights on. Lights on tall buildings disorientate migrating birds: sometimes mass collisions are caused by blinding or the inability to use the navigational adaptations in their eyes; in North America an estimated 4–5 million birds are killed this way each year. In England the crisis in songbird populations has been attributed to the loss of insects caused by artificial lights. Because of skyglow – diffuse luminance caused

by artificial light in ionised atmospheric pollution aerosols
– we live in perennial, or as David Bowie might have said,
serious moonlight.

Artificial light also creates new kinds of ecological
communities. A research project in Helston, Cornwall, famous
for its floral festival in May, counted the invertebrates associated
with streetlights 35m (115ft) apart over three days, and found
1,194 invertebrates belonging to 60 taxa (distinct groups),
which were far more numerous under the streetlights than
between them. Much greater numbers of harvestmen, ants,
ground beetles and woodlice were found hunting or scavenging
in the grass under the lights than were found in unlit areas; they
were taking advantage of the rain of bodies, killed, injured or
exhausted from flying too close to the light above.

I was at Shrewsbury Railway Station for an early train just
before dawn when my eye caught the iridescent purple shine
of a beetle on the platform. It was a dor beetle – a name that
means bumbling idiot – *Geotrupes stercorarius*, a black scarab,
25mm (1in) long, flying abroad late in the season to lay an egg
under a cowpat, which became befuddled by the station lights.
It may have detected the signals of hunting bats and dropped
to escape capture, or it may have beaten itself against the light
until it fell exhausted to the ground. Either way, the dor beetle
landed upside down and was crushed under a passenger's shoe.
It lay on the platform; life, luck, even the mites that infested
it, responsible for its other name, the lousy watchman, had
deserted it. Looking up, I watched *Araneus diademati*, European
garden spiders, centre on their webs around the beetle-
befuddling striplights under the roof above the platform. Each
light was occupied by two or three spiders; each spider had
woven an orb – a circular web of elegant simplicity consisting
of radial spokes of ampullate, dragline silk bonded by pyriform
threads at attachment points supporting gossamer spirals. The

inner spiral of smooth thread, the same ampullate material
as the spokes, began at the centre and opened outwards. The
second spiral of flagelliform silk wound inwards from the outside
edge, a more elastic aggregate thread for prey capture, covered
with globules of sticky liquid. This gossamer exudes rapidly
from spinnerets, glands that do not actually spin but secrete
silk by pultrusion, pulled out with a subtlety of force from silk
glands on demand. The silk produced at will is a protein syrup
that also contains sugars, lipids, ions and pigments that protect
the fibre. It sets on contact with the air, five times stronger than
steel, more elastic than a rubber band, tougher than Kevlar and
waterproof. Each orb wheel structure can be constructed in an
hour and typically contains 20–60m (66–197ft) of silk, weighing
no more than a milligram.

Each striplight spider had adopted the same head-down
position in the centre of the web. These were fully-grown female
orb-weaver Araneidae spiders, also called diadem or cross
spiders because of the baroque patterns of pearls on their orb-
like abdomens. These pearls are cells filled with guanine, the
substance whose name derives from its discovery in guano – bird
or bat excreta. The reflective and refractive properties of guanine
are found in many animals – butterfly wings, fish scales, beetle
iridescence, crocodile eyes and nightingale droppings – and
guanine has been developed for cosmetics, plastics and artificial
pearls. Spiders convert the ammonia produced in protein
metabolism into guanine; enzymes enable spiders to excrete
guanine, rather than uric acid as insects do, to retain water. They
can also store it, enhancing its reflectivity by separating it into
crystals in layers of amorphous guanine for lustrous display on
their bodies. Guanine molecules are one of the four building
blocks of DNA and RNA in nucleic acid, and it is now thought
they may have been formed in space, arriving on Earth via
meteorites. The orb-weaver spiders were waiting for telegraph

vibrations along the lines of gossamer that betray the presence of an insect. With startling speed, the spider will snatch the fly, immobilise it with a venomous bite and wrap it in aciniform silk to devour later. A male spider approaching the female may suffer the same fate before or after mating. Cocoons of tabuliform silk filled with eggs attached to station rafters are evidence of the posthumous success of some males. When the eggs hatch next year the spiderlings will sling a ballooning thread of ampullate silk into the air, and those not eaten by bats or swifts will join the aerial plankton in atmospheric currents until they find their own places to spin their webs. Meanwhile, at the height of their powers until winter claims them, the orb-weavers wait: sexual cannibals adorned in the extra-terrestrial glow of their pearl diadems, suspended in ethereal scaffolds woven from hundreds of glands controlled by their own sovereign will and unique metabolism, each silken thread silvered in the fluorescent glow – this was their garden of light.

Back in the lane, away from the streetlight, stars were out above the tall pines. Almost invisible bats zipped down the tunnel made by overhanging hazel and rising above high ground in the east the Moon was full. Seen through the shaggy boughs of an old larch or as central in the night sky as a spider in a web of light between the trees, the Moon had the strange allure that moths and bats and wanderers know. Clouds drifted across the lunar dial and its halo coloured like a bruise. This Harvest Moon was the closest it has been to the autumn equinox in the northern hemisphere since 2009; the next is due in 2020. Because of the slightly tilted orbit, it appeared brighter and the nights around it calmer. The old rhythms were out of kilter and the harvest had already passed by. It needed a new name, perhaps Orb-weaver. Just before the clouds thickened, the moon spun its own light garden and all who wandered abroad were enthralled.

<u>3</u> The Weedling Wild

ROSEBAY WILLOWHERB SEEDPODS cracked ajar like fans of white feathers. Exhausted after the carmine blaze of summer, the fireweed, rosebay, *Chamaenerion angustifolium* plants were dry, rusty and derelict. In that state, their long thin seedpods split into four strands, stretching open to reveal a mass of pappus – silky white plumes attached to up to 500 seeds in every pod. It has been estimated that each rosebay willowherb plant has about 80,000 seeds capable of being loosened by the slightest breeze – 80,000 aeronauts ready to drift away to found new colonies. These appear stuck.

Rosebay willowherb is a 1.20m (4ft) tall perennial herb with willow-like leaves and a spike of spiralling, rose-purple summer flowers. Its windborne seeds may travel 100km (62 miles) and remain viable for 18 months; its fleshy roots create a subterranean labyrinth that produces new shoots wherever nutrients exist, and even if broken up after 20 years will continue to develop the colony. It is a plant of wasteland – uncultivated, uncivilised, unproductive land, often the result of neglect, fire, disaster or some other kind of disturbance. 'What are the roots that clutch, what branches grow/Out of this stony rubbish?' asks T.S. Eliot in *The Waste Land*. Plants that clutch infertile ground often also colonise gardens, parks and farms, where they may be injurious to livestock, destructive to other plants, alien or non-native and so are described as pernicious or noxious weeds, invasive or undesirable plant species –

garden thugs. In ecology, wasteland plants are called ruderal
to describe their colonisation of disturbed land; 'ruderal'
comes from the Latin *rudus* or rubble, Eliot's 'stony rubbish'.
However, 'rude' may also be a way of describing plants
offensive to a traditional aesthetic that grew out of horticulture
and agriculture: weeds outside culture, without refinement,
of unruly behaviour, vulgar, harsh, uncouth, primitive. Rude
also refers to a robustness of condition and success – rude
health. 'Plants become weeds when they obstruct our plans, or
our tidy maps of the world,' says Richard Mabey. The weedy
wasteland, the ruderal habitats, are places that refuse to be
enclosed tidily; instead they become the obverse of cultivation,
outlaws infiltrating our maps along railway lines and motorway
central reservations, abandoned buildings, quarries, car parks
and security fences. Here the weeds remain shunned and
unappreciated; as Baudelaire says in *The Flowers of Evil*, 'Many
a flower casts away/Its sweetly scented fragrance on/The wastes
of deepest solitude.' Perhaps he meant something more human
by this, but it is a way of seeing the beauty of wastelands caused
by violence and sustained by neglect. It is also a way of valuing
them before they are 'found' and then lost to development.

Arrested in a kind of limbo, like a photograph, the rosebay
willowherb seeds had yet to liberate themselves and venture
into the wide world. Perhaps they first arrived in this rough
field in the slipstream of trains steaming along the line that
ran along its edge, now long abandoned. Before the railways,
rosebay willowherb was uncommon. Records of it only began
in the 18th century as a plant found amongst rocks and rubble,
forestry clearings after burning and in gardens. As if it had
been biding its time in obscurity, waiting, the building of the
railway network provided rosebay with a new world to colonise,
miles of stony rubble and frequent trackside fires took it to
every town and city. Then war liberated it: tree felling and

brash burning for timber in the First World War, the bombing devastation in Britain and across Europe in the Second.

If poppies in the fields of Flanders after the battles of the Somme and Passchendaele became flowers of remembrance for the fallen, then the fireweed or bombweed are flowers of remembrance for all the civilians that died in the bombing of London, Dresden and other cities. The lavish streaks of dazzling carmine in August became synonymous with both dereliction and school holidays.

Important for many insects, rosebay is the foodplant of the large elephant hawk-moth *Deilephila elpenor*. The scientific name means something like 'dreadful locust-thing' and newspapers often run stories about people who are terrified of its big, trunked caterpillar with intimidating eye-spots and defensively snakeish posture, which evolved to frighten predatory birds; the adult moth has a wingspan of 45-60mm (1¾–2⅜in), like a neatly folded, flying sunset with vivid rosebay-coloured markings. Although elephant hawk-moth caterpillars will also feed on bedstraws, *Galium*, its other foodplants are usually listed as garden species, so I wonder what this moth fed on before rosebay willowherb became so widespread. It would not be the first spirit of the wasteland to change its feeding habits.

Not long ago in this patch, I crept up on a butterfly, its wings flexing, pumping like delicate bellows as its proboscis sucked salts from dried dog urine. For a moment, I thought it might be a fritillary; the upper sides of the wings were a rich orangey-brown with complex dark markings, the kind of marmalade colours not seen since vintage cinema. The butterfly detected my presence and flew up powerfully, manoeuvred in a seemingly random pattern and then settled on a leaf. I could see by the shape of its wings, resembling the clipped edges of old bus tickets, that it was a comma butterfly.

The comma, *Polygonia c-album*, gets its name from the little white 'C' mark on the dead-leaf-camouflaged underside of its wings that looks like a comma.

The dictionary describes the comma as a phrase in punctuation that marks the smallest division of a sentence, the slightest interval or discontinuity; I was taught to read this as a breath, a pause. In the butterfly, the grimoire in its wing markings flashes an occult language only butterflies can read, and yet the closed wing moment of a comma-breath seems like perfect punctuation. The French name for the comma butterfly is *Robert le Diable*, which is also the name of a favourite 19th-century rose *Rosa × centifolia*, with a unique purple-cerise-scarlet-grey flower with wonderful old-rose fragrance, an opera about the moral redemption of the son of a mortal and a demon first performed in 1831 by Meyerbeer, and the father of William the Conqueror who was said to be the son of the Devil. I don't know how these demonic connections affect the comma butterfly but something strange happened to it. When growing hops – the comma's foodplant – declined early last century, it just about hung on around remaining hop yards of the Welsh Marches until, in the later 20th century, it suddenly began feeding on stinging nettle. Since then it has become one of the most successful butterflies in lowland England and Wales and its range has been expanding north at 10km (6¼ miles) per year. A Faustian pact?

Insects such as comma butterflies and elephant hawk-moths have extended their range because of climate change and the expansion of foodplants proliferating in unmanaged places around the county. Many of the most prolific species, proscribed in law, are fairly recent arrivals, such as Himalayan balsam, giant hogweed, *Rhododendron ponticum* and New Zealand pygmyweed, adapting to ideal conditions without predators, but others have been here for millennia and are now behaving differently. Some say rosebay willowherb was introduced from North America where it is a pioneer of forest fires, others that it is native to Britain; perhaps both stories are true but its history, its healing response to trauma and its spectacular flowers are revaluing previous prejudices about weeds of wasteland. Places John Clare called 'the weedling wild' nearly 200 years ago in odd uncultivated fields and 'baulks that lead a wagon-way', are now largely restricted to post-industrial, brownfield sites; these 'weedlings' present a vision of resurgent Nature. Rosebay willowherb was voted London's favourite wild flower in 2002.

A year later, another plant that thrives in the abandoned field next to the old railway line received its own, more dubious recognition: The Ragwort Control Act 2003. In summer, ragwort makes fields of gold and to walk in them feels far more transgressive than a bucolic stroll through wheat or barley. Unlike the pale, safe beige of ripening cereal crops, the ragwort is bold as brass. Unlike the slim pickings in the field stashes of mice (and men), the ragwort swarms with life. The insects, and those who feed on them, harvest a crop toxic to us and yet is the antidote to the intensive agriculture harmful to them. Ragwort contains toxic pyrrolizidine alkaloids that are dangerous if eaten by horses, ponies, cattle or sheep. However, in old herbals such as Culpeper's of 1653, common ragwort was used to cure the staggers and bot-worms in horses, and in people it treated eye inflammations, scrofulous tumours, burns, gripes, colic, sore breasts and scalded heads. Later works increasingly emphasised the toxicity to livestock, particularly horses, and in the culture of land stewardship and animal husbandry, ragwort became a sign of moral turpitude – what happened when we stopped sweeping out the corners. It is also a plant that has changed in recent decades, becoming even more prolific in defiance of being designated a noxious weed to be strictly controlled back in 1959.

According to the ragwort control code of practice, I can submit an injurious weeds complaint form about the ragwort in this field because it covers an area greater than 50sq. m (538sq. ft) so that the authorities can enforce the Act, force the land occupier to remove the ragwort by chemical spray, cutting, pulling or digging up and disposing of the plants as hazardous waste. I do not know who owns this particular patch, levelled from spoil heaps dumped here from a limestone quarry the other side of the old railway tracks many years ago, but I am very grateful for their benign neglect that has opened up a haven for wildlife – the occupiers that matter. The 1.2ha (3 acre) plot has gradually changed in character from limestone grassland, having not been grazed by livestock, only rabbits, for years. This year, it felt suddenly full of ragwort. A summer's day revealed comma, red admiral, meadow brown, common blue, gatekeeper, small heath and large skipper butterflies, their flight a folding-unfolding origami in the air. The cinnabar moth caterpillars, like items of lost games kit – a sock, a sleeve – in wasp-stripe warnings of toxicity, fed exclusively on ragwort leaves; the adults are burlesque black and scarlet day-fliers. A fantasia of hoverflies, robber flies, solitary bees, bumblebees and beetles fed on ragwort pollen and nectar. A harvestman – a full stop on improbably spindly legs – hunted ragwort visitors as did house martins swooping above. A flattened patch was evidence of a deer lay-up and dusk brought bats. There was more life in an acre of ragwort than in 100 acres of arable fields.

Senecio jacobaea, perhaps with something of the radical Jacobin about it, is the common ragwort, a dangerous daisy. 'Ragwort, thou humble flower with tattered leaves,' wrote John Clare in 'The Ragwort', 'I love to see thee come and litter gold.' The flowers are golden and glorious and its seeds, like those of willowherb and dandelion, float away on little feathery sails in their thousands. Perhaps because of its outlaw reputation as a pernicious weed, ragwort has an irrepressible spirit despite centuries of trying to root it out to protect livestock businesses – although there is argument about just how dangerous ragwort really is. John Clare's love of the ragwort 'waste of shining blossoms,' suggests an alternative account from the 1830s to the way it is perceived today, and I wonder what he would have thought about another ragwort that has taken to the railways to colonise the country: *Senecio squalidus*. Named by Linnaeus from samples taken growing on masonry, it did not become the squalid ragwort but named after the city whose dreaming spires it scrambled up – Oxford ragwort. Legend has it that a ragwort collected from the slopes of Mount Etna in Sicily, the active volcano that imprisons the monster Typhon, was taken to the University of Oxford Botanic Garden, where it soon climbed the walls. By 1770, a biennial, short-lived perennial or winter annual similar to common ragwort, but smaller, more open and adapted to volcanic debris, had colonised Oxford, and when the railways came it took off to become one of the most ubiquitous ruderal wild flowers of mass transportation, industrial revolution and war damage. *S. squalidus* may have evolved as a hybrid between two other Sicilian ragworts; it is a diploid plant with self-incompatibility, it cannot fertilise itself and so requires pollen from other self-incompatible plants to create viable seeds, and is studied to improve the understanding of how plants evolve to find new sexual partners and new places to colonise. Oxford ragwort flowers from May to December in railway ballast, walls and cracks in the concrete volcano of city heat islands that barely restrain the angry Typhon.

The other native injurious weeds on the official list to be controlled are: curled dock – a garden weed so tough it can survive being submerged in floodwater for eight weeks; broad-

leaved dock – a plant of waste ground and verges, the one you
rub on nettle stings; spear thistle – the robustly architectural
emblem of Scotland with richly imperial nodding bosses;
and creeping thistle – the smaller, pale lilac-tufted spoiler
of picnics and an arable weed. At the height of the summer
here, with rosebay willowherb and common ragwort in flower,
the jet stream divided Europe. As the south sweltered in
life-threatening temperatures, this side of the shower curtain
was cool, wet and, after Lamas on the first of August, full
of thistles. The rain had its own language: sometimes loud,
sometimes a whisper, but from downpour to drizzle, it spoke
of sedition, upsetting the established order. Rain hardened
the lushness and lustre of summer; the vegetation coarsened
into the green leatherette of dock leaves, exuding a stubborn
bloody-mindedness, thickening towards harvest time. In the
post-pastoral countryside, harvest seemed even more like an
insurgent Nature versus the occupying forces of agriculture.
Huge machines lay idle in sodden fields, half-cut, inebriate
with rain and what flourished most were thistles. 'Every
one a revengeful burst/Of resurrection,' wrote Ted Hughes
in 'Thistles'. When the Biblical Adam was ejected from the
Garden of Eden, his land was cursed, 'thorns and thistles it
shall bring forth for you; and you shall eat the plants of the
field,' (Genesis 3:18). In fallow, overgrazed, neglected land,
thistles are a mark of incompetence or poverty; when Nature is
not kept under control, thistles are a reminder of the Biblical
curse. It's the law. According to the Weeds Act of 1959, the
rapidly spreading root system of creeping thistle releases a
biocide into the soil that inhibits the growth of other plants;
spear thistle is severely competitive, eliminating pastoral crops
and opening other crops up to insect infestation. The 2014
updated version of the law explains, 'It is not an offence to
have these injurious weeds growing on your land. In fact, they

all have conservational benefits. However, you are responsible for controlling them.' Thistles, like sin, are still the subjects of a collective responsibility, which is now confused between agricultural efficiency and the protection of biodiversity; some may see the weedy wilds as evidence of moral decline, others as ethical progress for natural regeneration.

The little pappus parachutes of thistledown, each individual of tens of thousands, carry the plant's journey into the future on voyages to touch down in new places. Each seed may wait 20 years for the right conditions in which to germinate and when it does, colonisation is only temporary; its ascendency lasts until other plans oust it, scrub overshadows it or bulldozers, ploughs and herbicides wipe it out.

In sunshine, the sinful thistles are lively with butterflies, bees and hoverflies, and even in the rain with insects sheltering under their spiky protection, they scatter percussive notes of colour through the stiff verges. Purple flowers feel loaded with the uncanniness of the dog-days.

A couple of months after they had run away, I wandered along the rough field's edge when suddenly there was a movement across the path and something scurried into the grass. With a key, I poked open the sward to find a magnificent creature, muddied but with enough sheen to reveal it as the violet ground beetle (*Carabus violaceous*). About 25mm (1in) long, oval-bodied with an indigo-violet iridescence to the flattened edges of its abdomen and thorax, long legs and scimitar mandibles, the beetle had just dug itself out of the ground and was going hunting in the weedling wild. Only weighing 1g, but strong enough to lift something a hundred times heavier, the beetle is a quick and powerful predator of slugs, worms and other invertebrates and usually nocturnal. Although I enjoy the charms of goldfinch that come to pick seeds, the fugitive pheasants and young fallow deer that hide

out here, the fighting shrews and haunting owls, it is the violet
ground beetle that appears as the tutelary spirit of this place.

Thistledown – one of the libertarian fairy swarm – twisted
hopelessly around on a spider's web, straining to escape this
waste of 'deepest solitude'. Fog muffled nearby rumbles and
beeps of construction machinery at the sewage works behind
a dark wall of *Leylandii* trees. A black crow feather stuck
upright in moss. A white pigeon feather lay caught in a pad
of bird's-foot trefoil. A green woodpecker flew down from
the quarry with a rapid, high-pitched yaffle. A raven crossed
overhead, making four soft barks as if in recognition. Rooks,
worm charming in the park, rose together into the grey.
Agitated blackbirds and other anonymous little birds fussed
about in the hedge. The rosebay willowherb collected water
droplets from mizzle. Seeing the seedheads stuck, their pappus

plumes like wet feathers as if frozen in time, reminded me of
a poem by Peter Reading, 'That find of *Longisquama insigni*',
about the finding of the earliest fossil feather from a reptilian
creature that glided through swamp forests millions of years
ago, something that eventually flew into the future. The poem
ends with a quote from the 1st century BCE Latin elegiac poet
Propertius: *sunt aliquid manes* ('there are some ghosts'). There
are indeed ghosts here: creatures that are now exiled or extinct,
people who came and went with the railway, the future folded
inside seeds to be carried away on white feathers; it is the
season of ghosts. We misjudge the weedling wild if we think of
it only as a relic of the past. Beautiful, novel versions of it turn
up in street ends, traffic islands, abandoned fields – new places
of ignominy.

4 The Flow

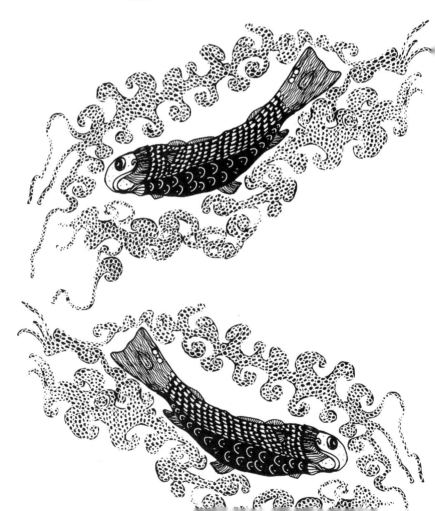

IT IS ONLY WHEN A SMALL DARK BIRD, its silhouette
darting over the water, turns to fly back, turns into the first
rays of sunlight through river fog, turns and sparks electric
blue, that I see it is a kingfisher. A moment of brilliance. 'Get
thee on boughs and clap thy wings/Before the windows of
proud kings,' wrote W.H. Davies, vagrant poet of the poor and
the wild, 'Nay, lovely Bird, thou art not vain;/Thou hast no
proud, ambitious mind.' For Davies, the jewel-like beauty of
the kingfisher comes from quiet places; it is not reserved for
the vanity of the rich; experience of wild Nature is real wealth.

Perhaps it is because I see kingfishers so rarely that
they make such an impression when I do, but the sudden
materialisation of the bird, first as a little dark figure in my
peripheral vision before a light switches on, is a flash of azure
in the grey waterscape, then an illumination. It is such a
distinctive experience that it can only be *Alcedo atthis* with
its metallic blue-green back and wings and flame-orange
underside. The vividness of kingfishers has singled them out,
their tropical colours over dour British waters gives them a
rare glamour and lends credence to legends of the Halcyon:
King Ceryx drowning in a shipwreck, his wife Alcyone dying of
grief, and the gods changing them into the Halcyon – mythical
kingfishers that nested on the Aegean Sea during the winter
solstice when the weather was magically calmed for them.
Halcyon Days are of fine weather when the waters are still –
days like this.

Down the steps from the English Bridge in Shrewsbury
to the towpath on a frosty morning, the Severn appears
impounded beneath smoky wisps of fog. Under a bridge
arch on muddy sediment where swans nest, now cleared
of vegetation but for a willow clump, a small tent has been
pitched, perhaps in the spirit of W.H. Davies. I couldn't
tell if it was inhabited but, looking at the water level, the
next rain in the Welsh Hills would wash it away. A couple of
weeks previously, I'd watched a man pull a salmon the size of
his forearm from this stretch of river with a rod. He passed
his phone to a homeless guy, who may have been living in
the tent, to take a photograph of the angler with his catch.
Technically, I'm pretty sure this was poaching and a rare
insight into secretive river-world practices that have been
going on for centuries, certainly for as long as people have
struggled against the territorial claims of others – maybe as
long as the oldest fish hook, 42,000 years. Despite the obvious
differences in size, poaching is an offence once levelled at
kingfishers, too. With a criminal disregard for property,
kingfishers take small-fry, minnows and tiddlers, from waters
in private ownership. Victorian fishermen ruthlessly persecuted
kingfishers with traps, others plucked their dazzling feathers
to make lures for fly fishing. Such persecution has a long
history. In Tudor times, a campaign to rid the countryside
of pests and vermin to promote a farming revolution passed
Acts of Parliament condemning wildlife, from foxes to moles,
ravens to kingfishers, to death and raised funds for bounties on
heads or tails. Gardeners, farmers, gamekeepers, water bailiffs
and churchwardens killed and encouraged the killing of wild
animals for centuries, hanging corpses on fences to advertise
their stewardship of the countryside, while their children threw
stones at kingfishers for fun, stole their eggs from riverbank
burrows and sold the feathered jewels for taxidermists to stuff

into curios of natural history, minus what W.H. Davies might see as the Zen-like humility of the kingfisher mind.

'It was the Rainbow gave thee birth,' writes Davies, 'And left all her lovely hues;' and in ways he may not have known, he was right. The shimmering metallic colours of the kingfisher are not produced by pigments but by the structure of its feathers that scatter light the way raindrops scatter sunlight into a rainbow. The kingfisher's flash is produced by the architecture of the bird's feathers. A vaned feather has a main shaft which has branches fused to it called barbs; these are branched again into barbules. Kingfisher feathers are divided into three groups: the orange feathers of its undersides contain pigment granules in their barbs; the cyan (greenish blue) feathers of is back and wings and the blue tail feathers do not. Instead, the barbs on these feathers contain spongy, keratinous nanostructures that reflect and scatter the short wavelengths in white light – the green and blue that produce turquoise, electric blue and aquamarine. The kingfisher would be dark brown, as I had first seen it flying through fog, if it were not for the Tyndall effect: short wavelengths of light reflect back to our eyes when light strikes a particle of equal or greater diameter to its wavelength. This is how blue light, like that of the sky, reaches our eyes from the spectrum. Cyan and blue are intensified in the kingfisher with the addition of broadband background reflection from the variable thickness of the cortex in the barbs of the shining feathers when they are illuminated from oblique directions.

The place in my eye where the kingfisher's image is brightest is the fovea – a central pit in the retina full of cones that concentrate the light, which is used to focus vision. Other animals have foveas in their eyes but birds such as raptors and kingfishers have two: a 'shallow' fovea that provides monocular, close-up vision; and a 'deep' fovea, at 45 degrees to the shallow one, that acts as a telephoto lens, magnifying the image to high resolution. This gives the birds a kind of binocular vision for judging the speed of fast-moving prey. Kingfishers perch on a branch or post above the water, moving their heads from side to side to alternate between fovea for near and distant vision to calculate when and where to dive for a fish. Their sight is adapted for underwater predation and yet their plumage – which hardly differs between male and female – has adapted for being highly, perhaps distractingly, visual. It is a thing of spectacular beauty but the Halcyon is a trick of the light.

Perhaps this is what Davies means in his poem by, 'And as her mother's name was Tears – so runs it in my blood to choose/For haunts the lonely pools, and keep/in company with trees that weep.' The rainbow giving birth to the kingfisher was not made of raindrops but tears, a deep melancholy through which natural beauty enters consciousness; a loneliness that hovers over an instinctive desire to withdraw from human society resonates with this cold misty morning by the river, home to the sudden flash of the kingfisher and then its disappearance into willows. As I walk, there is a slap on the water behind me. I spin around to see ripples widening from the spot where a large fish jumped. As the kingfisher appears to materialise from the river fog and flare into an existence seen by others, so this fish transgresses dark water for a moment in the light, making such a belly flop that I wonder what it communicates with above or below the water's surface. Of all the fish in the river likely to jump on a day like this, and big enough to make such a loud splash with ripples some yards in diameter, only the salmon seems likely. Why jump? There are few if any insects about to snatch from above; few if any predators likely to chase a fish this size – there are otters around but I haven't seen one in the water this morning. To make a mark, to taste the air, to see the light, to return from far away – why not jump? The Atlantic salmon's scientific name is *Salmo salar,* salmon leaper or salt-water dweller; salmon is 'salt man' in the local dialects where 'a' and 'o' are interchangeable – the Leaping Salt Man. Perhaps he saw the blue light of a kingfisher trace the surface, took it as a signal, a memory of home waters and jumped for joy – or something in the salmon psyche that amounts to the same thing.

When the clocks go back, the Salt Man leaps forward and time stops. On a fine autumn day – with high cloud in a Wedgewood sky, a brassy glow in the trees and a couple of days' worth of rain in the Welsh hills – the water pours over the Castlefields weir. The Severn crosses the weir in two steps: it licks smoothly over the lip, down a slope with a rough surface that makes dancing spiders of foam, then riffles taut and quick across a shelf to plunge into roiling white water before resuming composure downstream. A fish as long as my arm breaches the race. A missile of glistening skin and amber fin launches from the chaos in slow motion. The salmon leaps clear of history: clear of the bardic tradition of poets who venerated him because he went away and returned with the knowledge of the ocean; clear of the fishy stories of anglers and poachers who hunt him; clear of the river's power to send him back, to thwart his ambition. Part outlaw, part sacrifice, the poet Ted Hughes called him 'king of infinite liberty'. Above the weir's thunder I can hear Shrewsbury Railway Station. On the platform is a poster advertising the Heart of Wales Line with an image of a cheerful fishmonger holding a gutted salmon as if he's telling a joke: the Salmon of Wisdom. I recall the taste of salmon I ate yesterday and try to link it to the animal, now in mid-air, reading his own world by its taste. The olfactory rosettes are sensory organs inside the nares, the fish's nasal passages, responsible for relaying the molecular composition of death, life, danger and home to the brain. Just as minnows can 'taste' the death of another minnow in one part of the signature chemical in several million parts of water, so a salmon can detect a repellent given off by the skin of mammalian predators, such as seals, otters and humans; it is so sensitive it can taste the rinsing of human hands in the water. Sensing danger, salmon may hesitate at weirs until they feel safer, or the odour of bile acids, amino acids and calcium ions that recall the precise taste of the home stream overwhelms their fear and drives them to complete their journey. Despite the low levels of contaminants it takes to block the olfactory rosettes – industrial waste, sewage treatment, road run-off, pesticides, herbicides and fertilisers – that have flushed from the Severn's 11,420km^2 (4,410sq. mile) catchment, this salmon is alive to the flavours of place and the pheromone ribbons cast by the great hen salmon who swam upstream and are now scraping redds – nests in the gravel. He is propelled there by an instinct stronger than death and older than this river. The River Severn formed after the last Ice Age some 12,000 years ago, but the ancestors of the Atlantic salmon divided into separate groups 600,000 years ago in the northern seas, and their story is the journeys of glaciations, rivers, oceans, mountains and great forests. The Salt Man rockets higher to see beyond the weir's lip to the road of calmer water. What can he see with that fish-eye lens? Me with rapt attention watching his leap; others with cameras freezing the moment in time; all of us willing him over the weir, however desperate and hopeless his quest seems, we know his fame and future depend on it.

Although his eye has a mirror to pass light through twice to compensate for underwater darkness, it has the same rods and cones and principle chemicals that see the seven-colour rainbow spectrum as we do, but it contains a fourth chemical that grants the additional ability to see the ultraviolet range, too. His whole physical being is a sensory organ: he has a lateral line running down each side of his body containing neuromast hair cells that convert subtle changes in water pressure into electrical impulses, as our inner ear does, to orient himself in currents, elude predators, detect prey and swim together with others without colliding. He can hear sound that travels five times faster in water than it does in air. His heart responds to electric fields so that he may align himself upstream or downstream of an ocean current during his great wanderings. The salmon's wisdom patches into the Earth's magnetic field, using it as a map; magnetoception takes place when iron in his brain responds like filings aligning to the Earth's magnetic field for navigating his way back to the place imprinted in his nose to differentiate his home water from all others that lead to the Atlantic Ocean. The Leaping Salt Man is a probe voyaging in the Universe but despite his apparent liberty, his senses and memories tie him to a compulsion that reels him back to spawning streams as surely as any line hooked to his mouth.

Hatching from an egg laid in the redd, the salmon stayed in his birth brook for three years as fry becoming parr, feeding on fly larvae and avoiding other predatory fish and kingfishers, until he followed the tributary into the Severn and swam 160km (100 miles) to where the freshwater river becomes salt-water sea in the Bristol Channel. Here, as a smolt, this point on the electromagnetic map seared its coordinates into his mind for all the time he roved the Atlantic. After four winters at sea, surviving fishing fleets, porpoise, seal, cod, skate and halibut, the adult salmon – the grilse that can grow to 70cm (27½in) and weigh 51kg (112lb) – turns homewards. Fasting and fixated, all his senses drive him to cross the freshwater threshold again, heading for the redd scraped by a hen in the brook of his birth, waiting to lay her eggs when he can fertilise them with his milt. No time to rest, reeling to procreate his kind even if it kills him, he hangs in the air above Castlefields weir for a timeless moment as the watery circles of birth and death ripple beneath. He crashes onto the weir with a slap, rights himself and faces into the flow, defying the river for a few seconds before allowing himself to be cast backwards into the maelstrom. He tries again. Although it looks hopeless, his relentlessness comes from the knowledge that he can overcome all opposing forces, so long as he leaps time to a standstill.

Like the land and waters he travels through, the Leaping Salt Man is much changed by human history. The industrialisation and urbanisation of this and every other river catchment has so vastly altered ecosystems in recent centuries; the pollution, soil erosion and climate change that followed continues to unravel the very context of his existence; the release of farmed salmon has diminished the genetic range of the wild ones to such an extent that they are shadows of the ancient lineage moving through the shadows of an ancient world. Despite this, the salmon run, like the darting kingfisher, is a great affirmation of wildness in our time. 'I also love a quiet place/That's green/ away from all mankind;/A lonely pool, and let a tree/Sigh with her bosom over me', wrote W.H. Davies in 'The Kingfisher', and in the country or the metropolis, water and the flow of life, despite our destructive tendencies, is full of opportunities to see Nature.

Old Spear-face crouches in the rushes. The grey heron has folded itself – all beak and eye, wing and leg – invisibly for such a large bird, into the watery edge of a reedmace patch in a busy London park. Perhaps the people pretend not to notice the heron so the heron believes it really is invisible; they may steal a glance at each other from two different realities in the same place but their gazes never meet.

What crosses this divide between the heron's world and our own are the stories we tell of it. This is true for many other animals and plants and such stories include them, or perhaps appropriate them, into our reality, thereby stretching it towards theirs. The heron's world travels from the places Alfred Lord Tennyson describes in his poem, 'The Brook': 'I come from haunts of coot and hern...' 'Haunts,' it seems to me, mean something other than abodes, more a way of dwelling; the birds are spirits of wet, dank, secretive places that hold our origins, too. Tennyson's 'Brook', winds musically downstream from oozes, ditches, ponds and streams as a metaphor for the journey of a human life. But the flow of water, from its source to rivers, lakes, estuaries and what Dylan Thomas called, 'the heron-priested shore', transcends our mortality.

Old Spear-face now stands meditatively on the scaly green stick of one leg jammed into the mud of a canal called the New River. Built in 1613 to carry fresh water to London from the River Lea and springs along its 32km (20-mile) journey from Hertfordshire, the New River runs into Clissold Park in the Borough of Hackney. In the 19th century it also provided water for the aquatic theatre at nearby Sadler's Wells. Despite the strict management regime for metropolitan waterways – channelled above ground and culverted below – the New River is really part of a very old landscape and a hidden ecosystem. It became an ornamental canal in Clissold Park in the grounds of the 18th-century house, now restored and in public ownership. Today, people come to see fallow deer in a paddock, butterflies in a dome, budgies in an aviary and an enclosure inhabited by two goats, who look as though they've been rescued from some satanic ritual, while wonderfully exotic ring-necked parakeets chime from horse chestnut trees and conkers fall to the ground to be gobbled up by the goats. Old Spear-face is still. Its golden-ringed eye has a determined look, like that of the park's self-conscious cyclists, sellers of socialist papers, wedding photographers and food-stall vendors. Its wings cloak its body in plumelike tassels of grey. Slightly moving its head to watch for an eel or frog under the water's surface that reflects the finest autumn afternoon of high clouds and rumours of change in the trees, the heron sees through the membrane between a world we can see and an underwater world we can't. In heraldry, the heron often appears holding an eel in its beak, a creature plucked from the aquatic subconscious of these lands. How the heron catches the eel is key to how it is seen as a symbolic bird of omen and prophecy.

Stepping slowly into the water on long, spindly legs, armed with a spear-like beak and clothed in a cape of grey feathers, the heron's appearance suggests an archaic fisher spirit. Its hunting technique is to remain perfectly still, enduringly patient yet poised to strike at the slightest movement of eel, frog or duckling. In rock pool, saltmarsh, riverbank, lakeside, or fishpond the complete angler plays the waiting game. The collective noun for herons is appropriately, according to the medieval *Book of St Albans*, a 'siege'. The description may also go back to a legend that is the origin of the grey heron's scientific name: *Ardea cinerea*. In *Metamorphoses*, Ovid mentions the city of Ardea, in what is now central Italy near Anzio, south of Rome, whose inhabitants refused to surrender to the Trojans and waged war against them. Ardea was besieged and burned down, and from the ashes of its ruins flew a bird we now call the heron. The bird beat at the embers with its wings and cried with the agony of Ardea's people. The bird was lean, pallid, and because it was all that was left of the city, it was named after it: 'Ardea mourns itself'. The grey heron's species name *cinerea* means 'ash-grey': Old Spear-face is ominous. However, in the shared secret of the park, the heron appears neither ashen nor mournful.

The grey of the heron is more than a modulation between black and white. The artist, Bridget Riley, talks about 'the grey'd quality,' as an indeterminate nature of reality, something between stability and instability, certainty and uncertainty; she sees a 'pacing grey' as luminous disembodied light in steps or movements, such as ripples in water when, through art, Nature is 'an event, rather than an appearance'. In appearance, the grey heron plumage is identical in both sexes: each has a white head with a supercilium, a black bandit eye mask that becomes a crest falling in black aigrettes down the back; the beak is yellow-brown and the eye has a bright yellow iris. Chin, throat and neck are white to light grey tinged with buff at the base and broken by parallel black streaks. The upper back and hind neck are pale grey, the lower back and upper wings blue-grey. Like a shaman's cloak, the back has long narrow, lanceolate plumes. Flight feathers and upper wings are blue-grey to black with grey to white underwings. At rest, there is a black shoulder patch and white feathers at the bend in the wing. In flight, the broad wings are arched, the neck folds back like a cockpit and legs outstretch behind. The flanks are grey to white with white thighs. Legs are green-grey to yellow-brown. Herons are not really reclusive; they will roost in colonies they sometimes share with egrets or cormorants during rest periods at midday and after dark. Although British herons are non-migratory and tend to stay put, some have been found to travel to south-west Europe. Northern European birds will overwinter in Britain and some individuals may wander widely before and after breeding.

During the spring breeding season, the black aigrettes and long white lanceolate feathers on the neck and back develop fully, and the iris, bill and legs flush orange-red. It is at this time that herons are gregarious and nest in treetop heronries. 'Rwo-rwo' announce the males as they parachute down; 'arre, arre, arre' they shout on landing; 'clop... clop' snap the beaks of meeting birds; 'go – gogogogo' they alarm at unwanted intrusions; 'oooo' goes the aggressive forward stretch; and the youngsters' brass section tumults 'squawk, yelp, honk'.

The Mere at Ellesmere in Shropshire has an island formed
from road spoil dumped on the ice during the freezing winter
of 1812 when Napoleon was retreating from Moscow. The
trees on Moscow Island hold a heronry that is rigged with
cameras by the Shropshire Wildlife Trust so people in the
visitor centre can watch them. Heronwatch is certainly a way
that Nature shifts – to extend Bridget Riley's idea – from
appearance to event as art enables an intimate view of grey
heron life. For 25 years now, people have been able to watch
the heronry at Ellesmere through telescopes and live video feed
on indoor screens, as herons build and restore nests, breed,
incubate eggs and feed their young from February to early
June. The idea of camera access to bird breeding drama began
with the RSPB's protection of osprey nests at Loch Garten
in the Highlands of Scotland and later became a staple of
the BBC series *Springwatch*. This advance in natural-history
broadcasting has enabled a generation to see Nature in detail
that was only previously available to the most dedicated
naturalists skilled in fieldcraft. It is a kind of voyeurism in
which the wildlife subject is unaware of the human viewer who,
as the observer observed, is now part of a surveillance culture
that includes CCTV cameras in public spaces and reality
television in 'private' ones. Heronwatch and similar forms of
clandestine filming of animal behaviour feed an apparently
insatiable appetite for natural-history entertainment, which
may recruit advocates and funding for nature conservation, but
may also objectify Nature as a consumable resource. (It could
be argued that I'm feeding that appetite at this very moment.)
The popularity of modern wildlife documentary may seem
a far cry from audiences gathered for the spectacle of heron
hawking but it does share some aspects of our hunting history.

Perhaps because it is such a large bird, with a commanding
presence in the air and being a visually dramatic hunter itself,

the heron was considered the ultimate quarry in falconry. Hunted with casts of trained peregrine, gyr or lanner falcons by the highest levels of English aristocracy while spectators watched in awe, heron hawking was a medieval obsession that survived the switch to guns for hunting birds. This 'sport' still occurs in parts of Europe but despite conflicts with some fish farms, anglers and garden-pond owners, the grey heron is now protected in Britain and its population is the highest for centuries. These ways of seeing the heron as an object for our gaze to capture, or prey for our vicarious hunting desires through the proxy falcon, obscure the event of the bird as an omen or augury.

From an early age, I watched the ponderously deliberate flight of the heron and heard its 'frarnk!' claxon call through the air; to me these expressions were loaded with unknown meaning. There is something uncanny about herons. They haunt the primal watery places that have always sustained the physical and spiritual life of the community. They step slowly around us in a world that we have so altered yet they hunt and wait silently, fly and call enigmatically, roost and breed raucously, as they have done for millennia. They do so knowingly and without returning our gaze. Old Spear-face, looks very slowly this way and that, peering into the aquatic theatre of the New River, being very secretive. Hunched in its London pond it looks more like a Dickensian parlour lamp than an omen of impending disaster, and yet the city is always just a few wingbeats from catastrophe. The Great Fire, the Blitz, 7/7, Grenfell Tower, the ash of Ardea and the cry of its people are never too far away. Whatever the heron means to us, there is a place where the bird can open its wings, spanning 2m (6½ft), and stretch from bill-tip to claw into its own world; the grey heron has a balletic elegance and, despite the constant risk of stumbling into slapstick, becomes the harpoonist, reaching through its own spine to hurl the javelin of itself.

<u>5</u> Commons

LARKS RISE ON Minchinhampton Common. Daring
a breeze, emboldened by the first flashes of sunlight, the larks
ascend tentatively. Above cattle-grazed lawns, flapping flags
on golf greens, creaking hawthorns, old dug-outs puddled
with last night's rain; above the traffic noise and creeping
suburbanisation and a hum of pumps in the buried reservoir,
the larks open a little corner of their songs. Out tumbles that
wild, evocative voice from a countryside that barely exists
elsewhere now, a hopeful song.

Minchinhampton is 182.7ha (451 acres) of unfenced
Cotswold grassland. It has nine or so farmers with commoner's
rights to graze cattle, the oldest golf club in England, unique
wildlife and the half a million visitors who come to do what
people love to do on open, free, common land.

A hundred years ago, when the ink was still wet on the
deeds which passed to the National Trust from the estate of
eminent entomologist Thomas Bainbrigge Fletcher in 1913,
the poet Ivor Gurney, wounded on the Western Front in
France, imagined his ghost returning to the high commons of
his beloved Cotswolds in 'Above Ashleworth':

The Cotswolds range out Eastward as if never
A curve of them the hand of Time might change;
Beauty sleeps most confidently for ever.

Wandering over the bulwarks – a long arcing earthwork raised 3,000 years ago for a now-mysterious purpose – to a crossroads called Tom Long's Post at 600m (1,968ft) above sea level, the windy landscape encompasses woods above Thrupp; the Slad Valley; Golden Valley; Woodchester Park's wind turbine; Bussage, once common land now housing estate and Ozleworth's cold war surveillance tower. Commuter traffic crossing the Common, past battered milestones on the London Road, follow an ancient conduit of trade and wayfaring as butterflies drift over wild flowers and meadow pipits sing from bramble clumps. National Trust volunteers clear scrub to restore limestone grassland.

Although this is tied to an aesthetic ideal of wide-open space, scrub-clearing and grazing is what gives Minchinhampton Common its ecological importance. According to Matthew Oates, the National Trust's naturalist and butterfly expert, the story of the Common in modern times can be told through the story of the Adonis blue butterfly; for centuries little changed on the Common until the arrival of myxomatosis in the 1950s that decimated the rabbit population. By 1962, the Adonis blue butterfly had gone. Without rabbits, coarse grass ousted the horseshoe vetch the Adonis caterpillars ate and the butterfly, already at the northern reaches of its range, became locally extinct. Then, in 2003, the Adonis blue returned. Some suspected a secret reintroduction by butterfly enthusiasts but Matthew prefers the theory that a small population managed to hang on elsewhere in the Cotswolds and, taking advantage of climate change and conservation grazing, discovered its old haunts at Minchinhampton and began to thrive. The Adonis blue is a dazzling butterfly with lapis wings fringed with black and white. Other wonderful wildlife at Minchinhampton Common include the incredibly rare downland bee-fly, lizard orchids, pasque flower, Duke of Burgundy butterfly, and 50 greater and 100 lesser horseshoe bats, which roost in nearby quarry caves and hunt the Common for insects that rely on cow pats.

For now, at least, conservation subsidies to graziers keep the cattle on the Common, which supports wildlife and protects their ancient rights. High above the Stroud Valleys and Severn Estuary, these rights support Neolithic burial mounds, Celtic field systems, Iron-Age hill forts, Saxon ditches, ghosts of a highwayman's wife, kite flyers, horse riders, dog walkers, picnickers and bird-watchers against forces that would undo them. But for how long can Minchinhampton Common resist pressures for development all too visible nearby? And how sustainable is it? The skylarks hoist themselves into a clearing sky until they're just motes for performances in which they risk everything. They open the full drama of their songs as if from nowhere, high above the cattle and ice-cream vans, wild flowers and fluttering Adonises, pushchairs and dogs down below on the Common, and inspire new generations with a song which remains steadfastly full of hope.

This ancient association between people and commons is a kind of pact: irrespective of ownership, common land today is a relic of an ancient communal farming practice dating back at least to medieval times, becoming legally recognised with the Commons Act of 1285. Common land is privately owned but those people with traditional rights can work it for grazing sheep, cattle or horses, bring pigs to eat acorns, dig turves for peat or fuel and collect firewood, and forage for culinary and medicinal herbs. The continuity of these traditional practices, such as control of the number of grazing animals, the frequency of burning areas to restore grass, refraining from ploughing and fencing – maintained a landscape which then supported the people's rights, and indirectly wildlife, over time. Those who have these rights are known as 'commoners' and they often inherit their rights with the deeds to their property, a house on or near the common. The landowner retains other rights to the land, such as rights to minerals and large timber and any common rights left unexercised by the commoners. However, in legal terms, the situation is much more complicated with no single definition of 'common land', or 'common rights' or even 'common'.

The condition of common land is dependent on how commoners exercise their rights. In 1968 the American ecologist Garrett Hardin wrote an influential essay called 'The Tragedy of the Commons' in which he used commons as a metaphor for public goods and claimed pasture held by a group, where each individual can graze sheep, would suffer because the incentive to increase the number of sheep for the private gain of commoners would overwhelm the grazing capacity of the common. Something like that happened in the 1970s with EU agricultural subsidies leading to overstocking, overgrazing and severe damage to vulnerable ecosystems. The ravens, however, enjoyed a population burst due to the amount of available food from dead and dying lambs, afterbirths and sick sheep. Although the 'headage' payment for sheep has been scrapped and grazing has decreased, the opposite is now happening. Common land, all open to public access on foot by law, is in danger of disappearing through neglect.

'Our commons,' wrote John Clare in the 19th century, campaigning against their loss due the enclosures, 'are left free in the rude rags of nature.' That may not be as true now but there are still many places to experience that sense of freedom, that rough, untidy version of Nature; a community of wildlife, users and wanderers of commons, that gives these places such cultural, scientific, aesthetic and spiritual value. There is also an important historical feeling of solidarity with John Clare for ordinary people to maintain their common

rights, particularly against the enclosing of common land
by wealthy landowners for their private benefit, as in this
old rhyme: 'They hang the man and flog the woman, that
steals the goose from off the common, but let the greater
villain loose, that steals the common from the goose. The law
locks up the man or woman, who steals the goose from off
the common, and geese will still a common lack, till they go
and steal it back.' Despite the Enclosures Acts and centuries
of land-grabbing and fencing off, there are still 526,100ha
(1.3 million acres) of common land in England and Wales,
registered in over 9,000 separate units covering all types of
landscape and habitat, and most commons in England have
a national or international designation for wildlife, landscape

or archaeology. There are also commons with their own local or private acts of parliament, including the New Forest (approx. 22,000ha/54,363 acres), Epping Forest (approx. 2,500ha/6,178 acres), and 17 other kinds of commons, often in towns or cities, ranging from Mitcham Common in the London borough of Merton (174ha/430 acres) to Cassiobury Common in Watford at less than 1ha (2½ acres). The situation in Scotland is different. An Act of 1695 allowed common land to be divided between landowners; the lack of parish councils and municipal maladministration allowed private estates and farms, supported by the courts, to appropriate commons in Scotland. The threat to common land today is from creeping suburbanisation, particularly in the south of England where gardens, car parks, fencing for grazing and prettifying changes the nature of commons. Despite legislation, no one has a duty to protect them but there are still many that are nationally and internationally renowned for wildlife, such as the strange nocturnal churring of nightjars on Sutton and Hollesley Commons, Suffolk; the large blue butterfly, returned from extinction to Collard Hill, Gloucestershire; adders basking on sandy heathland of the Gower Peninsula, Wales; red deer roaring in the autumn rut on Dartmoor National Park, Devon; and the spring lek courtship displays of black grouse on the moors of North Pennines.

In 2009, the economist Elinor Ostrom won a Nobel Prize for her pioneering work on commons, on the common pool of resources such as water systems, the atmosphere and also knowledge, which need to be managed as public property. Ostrom says these resources may be more effectively used if they are held in common and regulated by custom and norms, as is common land, rather than using legal measures to mitigate the dangers of over-use or underinvestment – order without law. In a way, this is a good metaphor for the ancient commons; they are a kind of outlaw country, wild places each with its own character and ways of doing things. Commons have been teaching us about community for a very long time and they continue to do so when these ancient ideas are transposed into 21st-century life.

A little buddleia jungle flickers with small tortoiseshell, peacock and red admiral butterflies. The last of the speckled woods and a gatekeeper are dithering around black knapweed. Hoverflies and bees cluster on yellow candle-ends of moth mullein. Redwings roll wasps off crab apple windfalls, fieldfares pluck dog rose hips and goldfinches winkle seeds from teasels. Woodcock poke about here, deer come and browse, voles and mice stash their winter supplies in old drainage pipes. This place has a chequered past. At various times it's been a limestone quarry, a rubbish dump and a builder's yard. Now abandoned by people, it is full of wildlife and one of my favourite autumn haunts. Although far 'greener' than surrounding fields protected by planning regulation, this wildlife haven is vulnerable to being built on. This is a brownfield site.

The importance of brownfield sites for wildlife and open space is now well recognised but because of an assumption in planning legislation that to protect the countryside and the green belt around urban areas, brownfield sites must be the priority for development, they are currently at risk. According to the Forestry Commission, there are 66,000ha (163,090 acres) of brownfield land in England alone and one-third of this lies within Greater London. The government is committed to building millions of new homes on brownfield land by 2021 and so there's a conflict characterised by the conservation of wildlife and habitats close to where people live versus economic development.

An official definition of brownfield is: 'any land which has previously been used for any purpose and is no longer in use for that purpose,' and more specifically land that was 'occupied by a permanent structure and associated fixed surface infrastructure.' According to this description, Stonehenge, Tintern Abbey and many castles should be designated brownfield sites but because they have such archaeological and historical value, they are not. British culture has a passion for ruins. They are, according to Rose Macaulay, writing *Pleasure of Ruins* in the bombsite-riddled London of 1953, 'part of the ruin-drama staged perpetually in the human imagination, half of whose desire is to build up while the other half smashes and levels to the earth.'

This 'ruin-drama' also surrounds derelict tin mines, abandoned steel works, redundant shipyards, empty tower blocks and tracts of urban wasteland. The 'dark satanic mills' of the 19th- and 20th-century are being preserved for the future, converted into expensive apartments and offices, but it's unlikely many, other than a few ex-Ministry of Defence buildings, will be allowed to crumble into a ruinous state. These previously industrial, commercial, military or residential places referred to as brownfield become the focus of tensions between 'ruin-preservers', who want to protect scientific and heritage values and 'ruin-destroyers', who want to demolish and build something else. This tension is also complicated by the perception that ruins attract elements of social disintegration, such as vagrancy, drug misuse and violence, and also harbour dangers such as pollution, unstable structures and a morally repugnant untidiness. The 'brown' in brownfield implies contamination but there's also a cultural sense in which a best-forgotten past contaminates the future and somehow hanging on to derelict land stands in the way of progress.

Sometimes natural regeneration is the key to the future because so much of our industrial heritage is toxic. In hundreds of miles of waterways, coastline and hundreds of acres of land, soil and groundwater are contaminated with heavy metals, hydrocarbons, arsenic and biocides. Natural processes of micro-organisms, fungi and plants can break down, neutralise or store contaminants safely. Ironically, much urban greenspace is brownfield and provides the green networks on which towns depend. However, brownfield is not an exclusively urban phenomenon. The woods of the Severn Gorge at Ironbridge in Shropshire regenerated around the hellish foundries now called the birthplace of the Industrial Revolution; abandoned mine workings on Dartmoor are home to a huge colony of greater horseshoe bats; the drifts of mountain pansies in Upper Weardale, County Durham grow on highly poisonous spoil from lead mines; spoonbills in the reeds at Orford Ness in Suffolk fly over the 'Pagodas' once used for testing nuclear weapons. These are places in which the abandonment of industrial or military land created the space for plants and animals to establish and now they are managed for their wildlife importance.

When the military first came to Lodge Hill on North Kent's Hoo Peninsula 150 years ago to defend the Thames Estuary and therefore London, it found a remote, isolated place ideal for keeping secrets. It made and tested weapons and soldiers for all the conflicts around the world that Britain has been involved in and, as the mock-up of a Northern Ireland street testifies, conflicts nearer to home as well. Then, as feudal landlord, the Ministry of Defence decided to pull out of Lodge Hill and sell the land for development. After years of controversy, a public enquiry was held in March 2018 to decide whether or not to build 5,000 new houses – a town – on the 144ha (356 acres) of scrub, grassland and woods of Lodge Hill. This proposal was socially divisive locally and conservationists were alarmed at the potential loss of wildlife. However warlike the intentions of the Ministry of Defence, however lethal its bullets, grenades, explosions and whatever else, birds and butterflies thrived inside its fences. Most famously, Lodge Hill had the highest population of breeding nightingales in Britain.

Nightingales are adept at concealment; they are ventriloquists, throwing their voices from deep cover, understanding the power of a song to enchant is lost when the singer is revealed. A watchful bird may begin its beguiling song with a croaky creaking, a warning to other birds that someone is approaching its nest. Samuel Taylor Coleridge explained that nightingales sang not from the same kind of sadness as human hang-ups but from their own 'wanton tipsy joy'. Lodged in undergrowth, male nightingales remain inconspicuous while their song or 'gale' – *galan* is Old English to sing and *galinn* is Old Norse to bewitch – ventures into darkness as sonic beacons for enchanting female nightingales and, indirectly, human listeners. This combination of performance, beauty, romantic love and nocturnal vigil creates a mythic power that makes nightingales unique among songbirds. Its musicality may appeal to human senses but 'song' feels like a shorthand description of what the nightingale actually does. The sound comes from the syrinx, an instrument similar to our larynx but closer to the bird's heart, which produces an extraordinary range of high and low frequency notes. The nightingale's daytime song is beautiful enough but as darkness falls and other birds are hushed, the songs of a 'watch' of nightingales sounds as if the music of Persian rose gardens pours into the Kent Marshes. It is loud – at 90 decibels this song can resonate in a human chest. Computer recordings of birdsong can detect sounds of less than one-tenth of a second that human ears are unable to hear, but female birds certainly respond to these 'sexy syllables'. We may not understand nightingale song but it has an emotional effect on us that now carries a powerful message, a warning, something the poet Peter Reading described as, 'a cadence of ominous harmony... like a tolling'.

A nightingale sang with the cello played by Beatrice Harrison in her Surrey garden in 1924 and was the first live birdsong ever recorded by the BBC. In 1942, in the same garden, nightingale song was recorded with RAF bombers passing overhead; the surreal juxtaposition of the two sounds may have been wartime propaganda but it entered folk memory at a time of crisis. As a child growing up in Shropshire in the 1960s, I would go to Lloyd's Coppice in the Severn Gorge, woodland regenerated around Ironbridge and Coalbrookdale, birthplace of the Industrial Revolution in Shropshire, to hear the most northerly nightingales singing on summer evenings. They vanished decades ago; now I only hear them in their shrinking territory of southern England. No one knows precisely where nightingales go in winter but we know they travel here from sub-Saharan Africa. They are trapped and shot in Cyprus and Malta, and although Kent is a summer stronghold, their population is shrinking in Britain – probably due to things we do, such as changes in agriculture, land use, increased predators, development – and so they are vulnerable and threatened. In the thorny tangles of dog rose at Lodge Hill, the nightingales may sing their last if they are not saved from development. The need for new housing and jobs requires careful planning but nothing will compensate for destroying places like Lodge Hill and undoing our lamentably few conservation achievements. With the coming challenges to environmental protection and the opportunity of rewriting, even rewilding a British identity, it makes sense in my view to encourage a more creative approach to the common-wealth of wild life.

There are other, far more ephemeral, transitory places than Lodge Hill, which may never become protected nature reserves, and yet are very important refuges. In their 2012 book *Edgelands*, Paul Farley and Michael Symmons Roberts write lyrically about landfill, scrapyards, car parks, skip depots, industrial estates and gravel pits – 'part of the gravitational field of all our larger urban areas, a texture we build up speed to escape as we hurry towards the countryside, the distant wilderness'. But it is the 'edgelands,' as new stages for ruin-drama, which create the wonderfully wildlife-rich places described by Richard Mabey in his 1973 book, *The Unofficial Countryside*.

Because of the ecological unravelling of much of the countryside, some species now depend on 'surrogate' habitats provided by brownfield sites. The Thames Terrace grassland habitats of the brown-banded carder bee and the shrill carder bee have been lost to development, stabilised river cliffs and constructed flood defences; they now depend on brownfield in the Thames Gateway. A moth called the small ranunculus, thought to have disappeared from the UK before the Second World War, has recolonised brownfields in England and Wales. Other moths, such as bright wave, chalk carpet, wormwood and six-belted clearwing rely on brownfield sites. Silver-studded blue butterflies continue their complicated affair with ants protected by the concrete runways of disused wartime airfields, and dingy skipper butterflies need the open warmth and bird's-foot trefoil found in abandoned quarries. In fact, 15 per cent of all nationally important insects are recorded on brownfield sites. According to the invertebrate conservation charity Buglife, brownfield has as many red data and nationally scarce invertebrate species as ancient woodland. Many of these species require the constantly shifting opportunities of 'transient' habitats. As Rose Macaulay said, 'ruins are always on the wing'.

Dereliction is not the sole qualification for brownfield. Railway lines with their cuttings and embankments, motorway verges, canal towpaths, retail parks, open space backed on to by housing estates and enterprise zones – unlike the proper definition, these are all places functioning as intended but with unintended wildlife importance, and because they are urban or industrial they are also regarded as brownfield. Everything we build or knock down, dig up or fill in, manufacture or discard, creates an opportunity for something, an 'equivalent' habitat to a wild one. A pile of bricks or stretch of asphalt is equivalent to open, heat-retaining heathland for basking common lizards. Rubble on roofs or car parks offers an equivalent to mountain scree slopes for black redstarts hunting spiders. Warehouses in docks act as sea cliffs for nesting seabirds. Railway ballast can stand in for limestone grassland, and so on.

Human activity creates new forms of contamination. Much work has been done to show how street trees, urban forests and sustainable drainage techniques help to ameliorate the effects of atmospheric pollution and climate change. Less is known about the effects of microwaves, radiowaves and electromagnetic radiation on house sparrows and bees for example, and I have written elsewhere in this book about the influence of artificial light (see Chapter 2).

One of the most toxic legacies of industrialisation is social deprivation. In many post-industrial areas, ecological restoration is being linked to social regeneration, community welfare and individual health. In many towns and cities these ideas are rolling into something called urban commoning, a new way of combining participative politics with environmental sustainability. As public services become further stretched and threatened by austerity measures and urban development is controlled by large corporations, community-owned, or community-controlled land, such as allotments, gardens, urban greenspace, micro farms and recycling centres form an important kind of common land. This way of working

urban land and brownfield sites may not easily reverse the
18th-century enclosures and transfer the equivalent of
commoners' rights to graze livestock to the landless working
class because, as Ostrom said, the commons require a common
strategy for managing it; the model for understanding this
is now more like Wiki-style information-sharing and social
media than exclusively land containing environmental
resources. However, the ecological quality of brownfield sites
is a common good, of vital importance to public wellbeing,
and implies a shared existence with lives intrinsically valuable
in themselves.

The raven is a commoner returned from exile to claim her
ancient common. She flies over Catherton Common on the
Clee Hills, over my little buddleia thicket in the old builder's
yard and rubbish dump, and on to a copse with a few trees
and nettle patches surrounded by housing in Wolverhampton:
these are places of immense value to the people and wildlife
who live there but they're also part of a wider network
connecting through conurbations. These connections prevent
the disintegration of isolated fragments of habitat and connect
human communities, too. In south Essex, conservation bodies
are protecting the habitats of viviparous lizard, adder, great-
crested newt, water vole, five-banded weevil wasp, turtle dove
and black-tailed godwit on old gravel pits and Thames Estuary
salt marsh, such as Canvey Wick and Wat Tyler Country Park.
There are similar projects in Teeside and Falkirk. Wigan
has a landscape-scale initiative linking nature reserves and
open space on areas of mining subsidence, and coal spoil
throughout the city, with room for sailing and motorcycle
scrambling, as well as water shrews, water rail and hopefully
soon, breeding bitterns booming in the reedbeds. Other
important brownfield sites that are now commons by virtue
of them being reclassified as nature reserves include: Orford

Ness, the mysterious, weapons-testing site on the Suffolk coast; Camley Street, recolonised coal depot for London King's Cross Railway Station on the Regent's Canal; Saltholme, a salt marsh bird reserve surrounded by oil refineries on Teesside near Middlesborough; Gwaith Powdwr, a decommissioned explosives works above Porthmadog on the Llŷn Peninsula; Kinneil Colliery near Falkirk in Scotland and the land along Bo'ness Harbour. Commons, whether green or brown, legal or outlaw, fenced or free, are the almost-wild antidote to the private enclosure of public space. Commoning is the verb that will describe the way the landless return to dwell in their land; the geese will 'steal back the common'.

6 Wild Moors

'GO BACK, GO BACK, GO BACK!' There is an old scratchy gramophone quality to the grouse's complaint, a voice clipped and urgent, like a radio announcer from a bygone era. The bird warns us to leave the hills and return to our own world. Ironically, the natural beauty of the red grouse's heather moorland we seek for solace, space, vista, freedom and wildness is as dependent on human ambition as the towns we have come from. Up on the Long Mynd in the south Shropshire Hills, the Wild Moor is rippling under the hazy light of early spring towards the silhouette of the Devil's Chair on the distant ridge of the Stiperstones.

'Where's the Devil's Chair?' asked the man, as we scrambled up the rocks into the Stiperstones' throne-like tor of shattered quartzite last summer. 'This is it,' I said, 'you've found it.' 'But how do you know?' he asked incredulously. I tried to explain that it said so on the map and I'd been coming here for 30 years. There is something you just 'know' about the Devil's Chair on the Stiperstones that defies explanation. Despite the maps, legends, folklore and literature, this remarkable place has a strange, compelling identity of its own. When you go there you know what it is. The man relayed what I'd said to the rest of his family and they repeated it. 'But there's no sign saying this is the Devil's Chair, and anyway it doesn't look much like a chair,' he insisted. Perhaps they had expected smouldering red draylon and sulphur candles, but the man and his family didn't look convinced or particularly interested by this craggy phenomenon. They did not see the hobby falcon blading through the sky hunting small birds. They did not see the little flock of redpoll take fright and hide in a hawthorn tree. We said it looked more like a chair from a distance; they shuffled about in the heather for a while but after that they moved on. Maybe they would have been more impressed if there had been a sign and an interpretation board with a quote from the Shropshire novelist Mary Webb, who said of the Devil's Chair in her 1920s novel, *The Golden Arrow*, 'Nothing ever altered its look. It remained inviolable, taciturn, evil. It glowered darkly on the dawn; it came through the snow like jagged bones through flesh ... For miles around, in the plains, the valleys, the mountain dwellings, it was feared. It drew the thunder, people said.' Sometimes, you cannot find the Devil's Chair until it finds you.

'Go back!' The grouse gave its wind-up call from the heather and bilberry – known as whinberry in these parts. A tragi-comic bird: I admire the brown-hen sturdiness of red grouse, *Lagopus lagopus*, the moorcock's fortitude to endure tough hill winters, their whistling flight – fast and agile as a hawk – and their scarlet eyebrow combs that make them look fierce and astonished at the same time. These are indigenous British birds, found in the hills of Britain and Ireland where they feed primarily on the leaves, shoots and flowers of heather, other mountain plants, berries and occasional invertebrates. Their exclusiveness as game birds emerged from medieval arguments about the rights to own wild animals. As *ferae naturae*, wildlife belonged to no one in particular but all men had dominion over Nature. Although there was not universal agreement, the idea of game – animals hunted for sport or food – becoming the property of the landowner and cultivated for hunting gained traction. Hunting and falconry were English obsessions and the level of engagement in these practices defined social status. Despite public opinion mobilised by poets against animal cruelty and bloodsports, many species of wild animals began to disappear during the 17th and 18th centuries because of overhunting, game control or forest clearance and marsh draining. By the beginning of the 19th century, once common animals became scarce, such as eagles, bustards, goshawks, marsh harriers, hen harriers, ravens, osprey, cranes, kites, buzzards, ravens, wild boar, pine martens and polecats. By Victorian times, killing large numbers of small birds for food, as practiced elsewhere in Europe, had faded away and the concentration on shooting certain kinds of game bird using particular codes of behaviour became a privilege of the aristocracy and landed gentry. Country estates entertaining shooting parties on their moors still celebrate the Glorious Twelfth, the start of the shooting season on 12 August.

Grouse shooting became an important industry in the 19th century, exploiting Britain's 75 per cent of the world's total of heather moorland. Reports of 47 brace (94) of red grouse bagged (killed) here on the Long Mynd on one day in 1869 pales into insignificance when compared to Major Arthur Acland Hood's record bagging of 2,843 grouse on Broomhead Moor in the Pennines in 1916. The eccentrically British grouse is honoured or cursed, depending on your perspective, for its style of flight that makes it challenging to shoot – which qualifies it as sport – and the premium paid for its exclusive culinary value – which qualifies it as food. It is only found in some of the most beautiful landscapes in the country – which qualifies it as native. On grouse moors the vegetation is controlled by rotational burning to regenerate the heather and prevent regeneration of woodland. Moorland landscape and its ecology were shaped around game birds, reducing or removing competing species and predators. Shooting estates became an extremely lucrative business for landowners with vast holdings in the hills where only sheep farming and the remnants of quarrying and mining industries were viable. Today grouse shooting appeals as an activity for wealthy corporations as well as the traditional huntin', shootin', fishin' sector of society; it provides £150 million to the economy and employs 2,500 people; guns pay thousands of pounds for a day's shooting and are charged £150 for a brace (pair).

A few ravens were giving short fast 'kronk!' calls as they rattled around the sky. These birds would have been shot or poisoned and had been extinct on these hills for a hundred years until their return in the 1980s. Despite legal protection, illegal killing of raptors and mustelids persist in many parts of the country, including shooting estates not too far from here. Hen harriers have still not returned to this part of the Welsh Marches; goshawks and peregrine falcons have been found poisoned. During the 19th century, local field naturalist and ornithologist William Edmund Beckwith (1844–1892), wrote observations and reports of other game birds in the hills of south Shropshire. Beckwith claimed two great bustards were seen on the Long Mynd 60 years before his time, and black grouse, blackcock or heth cokk used to be very common in this area – they have not been seen here for generations. The nearest black grouse, *Tetrao tetrix*, in the Berwyn Mountains of Wales to the west, would now be lekking: the splendid black, white undertailed, red-combed males dancing in their arena for the females while the sky glows in oranges and browns. Beckwith noted that in the 1850s the hen harrier, *Circus cyaneus,* was once fairly common in Shropshire and still shot in the hills I'm walking in now, but in his day was seldom seen.

Out there, low sun illuminated high moors with no tangible focus, in a way that defied interpretation but held the windsweep of melancholy. Ghosts of animals and hill folk, miners, shepherds, keepers and whinberry pickers wandered the shadows below the Devil's Chair.

'Ghost' suits the hen harrier well. The male I saw flying over moorland on an island of the Inner Hebrides was like the one described by naturalist poet Colin Simms in his *Hen Harrier Poems* (2015), 'suddenly over the crest 'the blue hawk' swinging/in and away through all what had been still'. He was ghostly blue-grey with black wingtips, his owlish head more forward-facing than falcons and his flight uncannily light and quick, a heartbeat above the heather. The female is banded brown; they are 50cm (19½in) long with a 1.1m (3½ft) wingspan; like grouse, they nest in the heather; their skydance appears to be a telepathic choreography of aerial manoeuvres that often includes the swapping of food between talons; they feed on voles and small birds, such as pipits, waders and young grouse. After many millennia, this old predator/prey relationship has driven the hen harrier and the red grouse into an unlikely alliance. Many people now feel that the only way to save the hen harrier from extinction, from becoming what Simms calls 'a parable', is to ban driven grouse shooting. This is controversial and despite the efforts of sporting and business interests to object on resource-management grounds, the argument that heather burning contributes to climate change, draining increases flooding and illegal species control is causing extinctions has become a campaign that, like the one that banned fox hunting, now feels unstoppable. Up on the Long Mynd, 487m (1,597ft) above sea level, on the high heath of the Wild Moor is a place called Robin Hood's Butts, named after the 'butts' where the shooters hid as a line of beaters drove zig-zagging grouse from the heather towards them. Behind the butts are burial mounds, Bronze Age tumuli, round barrows, fairy tumps sacred to people here 5,000 years ago when the removal of woodland and the establishment of heath maintained by burning and grazing, created the dominance of heather or ling, *Calluna vulgaris*, together with whinberry, cowberry and cranberry and the equally enigmatic insects, such as the huge emperor moth and the ginger-bottomed bilberry bumblebee. We have come to regard treeless hills and mountains covered in heather or purple moor-grass, *Molinia caerulea*, as natural, but this is to deny centuries of labour keeping them thus. The possible rewilding of these moors is a vision for the future shaped by projects around the country.

Golden plover, a flock of 30 or more, stand in a patch of burned heather by the side of an ancient track across the Wild Moor as if waiting for a bus. Tempting as it is to scare them into the air to see the golden flashes of their underwings against a clear sky, we give them space to rest. Around the quietly waiting birds the light is momentarily fierce; it glitters emerald on the moss, and silvers tussocks of rush. The heather appears dark and lifeless with only the ghosts of last summer's flowers. Heather beetles and a phytophthora that has become a pathogen of whinberry are troubling the dominance of these two defining plants but today the sunlight bronzes their wiry stems, making them appear as if they are on fire. Like other hills in the Welsh Marches panorama, the Long Mynd is a hazy, indeterminate place between south Shropshire and the Welsh border. The 25.7km (16 mile) ridge, with its folds and plateaux, valleys and hollows holds species that only occur much further south, and has been officially designated as heathland rather than moorland. Some 2,226ha (5,500 acres) of the Long Mynd is managed by the National Trust as a nature reserve, working to restore it from years of overgrazing by sheep that held back the regeneration of heather and whinberry and reduced the numbers of rare insects and birds. Removal of all sheep would cause the hill to scrub over and

heathland species would be lost; so too the landscape character of open hills. This may change due to political and economic moves in the next few years and there will be a debate about whether the moors should be wild places, or even rewilded places, with the return of extinct species or whether they should be further exploited for their resources, agriculture and leisure developments. People with commoners' rights to graze sheep and ponies see their livelihood, their culture and their homes threatened by changes to the landscape brought about by outsiders who don't believe their traditional methods of burning and grazing work for wildlife.

Down in the historic beauty spot of the Carding Mill Valley, groups of schoolchildren chased stonefly nymphs in the stream. Day trippers peered through binoculars, took photographs or picnicked in the heather, where green tiger beetles stalked, wheatears flashed their white backsides and grey wagtails bobbed on stream rocks. At the head of the valley, the Light Spout waterfall, a 6.1m (20ft) high, mossy opening, poured out the wild song of the western hills. To stand in the stream under the Light Spout was to be drenched in sound and mesmerised by light. Through a narrow cleft, water gathered from sphagnum bogs with insectivorous sundew and butterwort plants on the Long Mynd's plateau, and plunged over the rockface into a shallow pool, before roiling down the stream of Carding Mill Valley, passing the old woollen mill – now a café and visitor centre – towards Church Stretton. Shale ledges broke the flow of water; it was spun into a million bubbles filled with light so that, on a day like this, it looked like a shimmering apparition. In time, the sound that was, at first, all roar and splash became clearer and I began to hear how the higher treble of the upper waterfall comprised hundreds of momentary notes shaken together by the energy of the flow into the lower bass notes of its entry to the pool. Like listening to music or birdsong, it became obvious that I was only picking up a fraction of the range of sounds at different frequencies and speeds transmitted by water pouring over stone. The more I heard, the more I listened. As my senses were taken over by the Light Spout, there were other sounds behind me in the valley that had grabbed my attention on the way to the waterfall but which I could no longer hear. Soft barks of ravens circled the hilltop; first there were five, then ten, and then 20 or more. They were youngsters gathering perhaps around a corpse or, because they began to disperse, waiting for something to die. Grey wagtails ticked away a thousand moments of the stream and a dipper flew from under a wooden footbridge. Guarding the valley was a stonechat in his bandit mask, a heathen on the heath. At the foot of the Light Spout, what I heard was a waterfall, what I listened to were the drifts of rain, deep soaks of moss, wings of birds, hooves of sheep, erosion of shale and water moving everywhere.

7 The Greenwood

'TZEEEP! TZEEP-ZEEP! TZEEEP!' When I heard the robin's alarm call I stopped on the old railway line and peered into the trees. Green leaves, green shadows – all the visual detail overwhelmed by the little sound. It had all the qualities of alarm that we recognise: an annoying insistence, a way of filling space with inescapable noise, an instinctive understanding that something was wrong. Like heart-monitoring machines in hospital, a reversing lorry or a distant ambulance, the robin's call was a warning, but unlike mechanised alarms it was also a narrative, comprising rapid, urgent phrases, as sharp as rattling a box of knives. The woods were a mass of verdure that merged to form the vanishing green into which everything disappeared – leaves, stems, trunks, brambles, ferns, shadows… Something stirred in a crab apple tree on the bank below and the alarm took shape, flashing red for danger as the robin turned.

The robin had not yet seen me; he couldn't see behind him, and although he had some forward vision, it was by using his excellent lateral view that he now fixed me with the gaze of his left eye. I think it is folklore that makes me think of him as male but in fact the sexes look alike. He continues to watch me with his left eye; the other he uses for navigation. Early experiments into robin migration put birds prior to migrating into an orientation cage and found the direction they fluttered in was that of their travels. When this took place at night it was assumed the birds were navigating using the stars, but when they flew in the same direction in a total blackout it was obvious there was something else involved. When the cage was surrounded by electromagnetic coils, the birds became disorientated. It was eventually discovered that robins orientate using the Earth's magnetic field, as do some other mammals, butterflies and fish. In the robin's case, it seems he has crystals of magnetite around his right eye and inside the nasal cavity of his beak. Together the two produce an electromagnetic map and compass. The birds are able to 'see' the Earth's magnetic field in relation to contours and edges in the landscape and the contemporary view is that a combination of chemical reactions and magnetite receptors helps them to navigate.

It is often thought that British robins do not migrate, that they are faithful to their neck of the woods all year round. It is true that the majority of birds remain within a short distance of their birthplace, but some robins fly to Spain for the winter, while some have places in Britain they go to in cold weather, returning to breed in the same place the following spring. Robins that fly in on the east coast in winter may be on their way from northern Scandinavia to breed in the Low Countries. Much about robin travel remains unknown, and birds that have been ringed to track their movements are often only recovered because they've been killed by cats or cars; they rarely live longer than two years. Robin travels may not be as epic as swallows, geese or terns, but they have an itinerant culture, a way of belonging to multiple places linked through intimate threads of robin history like ley lines. The constant garden familiar may not be the same one seen last year, may not be the same one seen in winter. Robins are spirits of the greenwood, and wherever that exists, so do they.

The alarmed robin in the crab apple tree paused to keep an eye on me. He thought I was a pig. One theory that addresses the question of why robins seem so tame around humans is that they adapted to the behaviour of wild boar. The snouting, grubbing and wallowing of wild boar on the woodland floor provides opportunities for birds to feed on invertebrates in deep leaf mould and soil underneath vegetation. Robins following boar soundings would not go hungry if they were quick and kept their nerve. People behave in a similar way to pigs through foraging and cultivation and gardeners delight in the robin perched on a spade handle taking worms by hand; they admire its courage, friendliness, modest beauty and its fierce defence of place. Male robins, far from being greeting-card symbols of peace and goodwill, can and do kill each other over territory.

Our instinctive, emotional connection with cultural values places robins at the core of a British relationship with Nature through which concerns for civilisation, cultivation and conservation are expressed. When William Blake wrote, 'A Robin Redbreast in a Cage/Puts all Heaven in a Rage,' in 1803, he drew on a figure already rich in folklore and symbolic of the harmless, innocent little friend – a wild creature that became an honorary pet. Blake was drawing attention to the common practice of trapping wild birds, clipping their wings and slitting their tongues to sing in cages as household pets, but he was also making the point that cruelty to animals and enslaving Nature for human amusement was synonymous with slavery, the oppression of the poor and the denial of liberty. Even during Tudor purges on wildlife as vermin, to kill or harm Robin Redbreast would bring bad luck; the Jacobeans called it the bird that 'best of all loves man', a pious bird with a myth of obtaining his red breast from the blood of Christ's crucifixion when he attempted to remove the nails, and thus became almost sacred and regarded with cautious respect. Tales of robins burying those who had died alone in the woods under moss and leaves – such as in *Babes in the Wood*; stories of the robin as the Oak King of the waxing year who usurps the Wren, the Holly King of the waning year, on the winter solstice – suggest an ancient psycho-spiritual role for robins. This legacy may have much to do with the way that the robin travels between two idylls: the garden and the greenwood and in a special way, unites them.

Robin Hood of Sherwood Forest, who may or may not have been a real character, who may or may not have robbed from the rich to give to the poor, seems not to have had his origins in mythology. Robin Goodfellow, the Puck of English folklore, appears in Celtic and Nordic languages and Shakespeare's *A Midsummer Night's Dream*; he is a pixie, hobgoblin, Pan figure and associated by Karl Marx with workers' revolution and did have mythological origins. What Robins Hood and Goodfellow share with Robin Redbreast is a woodland habitat of the imagination: the greenwood. It is here that the transgressive, outlaw, erotic, dangerous and rebellious spirit of British identity runs free outside the jurisdiction of civilisation.

Under the greenwood tree
Who loves to lie with me,
And turn his merry note
Unto the sweet birds throat,
Come hither, come hither, come hither:
Here shall he see
No enemy
But winter and rough weather.

WILLIAM SHAKESPEARE, *As You Like It.*

The greenwood is mythologised woodland, a secular sacred place, a hunting ground and sanctuary that may have emerged in opposition to Norman forest laws and other rights of ownership but is not restricted to the past or the countryside.

Now the greenwood exists in the cultural framing of liberty expressed through ecological relationships between its plants, animals, fungi, spirits, ghosts and ourselves – wherever we come from. Outside the woods, the world changes fast, accelerating without regard to seasons, weather or natural processes, with no way to arrest or relax the perpetual motion of careering time, the Anthropocene of climate change and species extinction. Inside the woods, there is a profound, if tenuous, relief from the urbanised, industrialised, militarised world outside. This feeling of refuge may be a conservative reaction that plays into post-Brexit ideas of British identity, but the greenwood also echoes with a revolutionary view of community in Nature: an environmentalist, locally distinct, self-governing, supportive society. Much of the greenwood virtues are currently expressed through medicalised notions of wellbeing. Forest schools reconnect children suffering from Nature Deficit Syndrome; green gyms provide therapeutic exercise through woodland management; the health benefits of a walk in the woods is supported by what the Japanese call *shinrin-yoku* – forest bathing: the phytoncides produced by trees to control microbial predation reduce depression and improve mental health in people. Trees affect the parasympathetic and sympathetic nerves; they increase the production of serum adiponectin, a hormone responsible for combating obesity, diabetes, cardiovascular disease and metabolic disorders. Although this may sound like the justification of woodland protection as a pharmaceutical resource for personal self-interest – more anthropocentric narcissism – the greenwood still exerts a powerful social influence. The outcry when government proposed the sell-off of publicly owned forests and woods surprised the country. Loss of public woodland is still happening by stealth, but the protest touched on a social need that can only be met by trees.

From tall lime trees above thorn and briar tangles at the top of the Edge, the view opened towards mountains of the west, a landscape of big fields to be harvested and tilled and reseeded and sprayed... There was a subtle echo of seasonal change seeping into tree leaves that occupied that industrialised expanse of land as an anarchic grid of oak, ash and thorn in hedges and open fields, copses, spinneys and woods; this arboreal framework held the idea of the greenwood together. From that vantage point, it was possible to feel the extent of the web of trees and woodland that moved across the land from countryside into towns and cities, into the dystopian pastoral of the urban forest, connected by water, soils, roots and fungal threads below and above by sunlight, rain, breeze and birds. The living map of trees spread out in a way not possible to see inside the myopic intimacy of the woods.

'Tzeeep! Tzeep-zeep! Tzeeep!' The robin was joined by other alarmists but I was not the cause of their concern. For the briefest of moments, I saw what they were agitated about: the barred feathers of a tawny owl, taking its chance to escape the mob, gliding into shadows full of life and story – the vanishing green.

Lords and ladies, cuckoo pint, Jack-in-the-pulpit – these names are medieval nudges and winks about genitalia and copulation that have survived in contemporary ecological literacy. They belong to a trick flower, an arum with mottled spear leaves that jumps out of the earth with a bawdy humour that mocks the righteous and revels in the rude. This irreverence is minor compared to that applied to the apparition that is first encountered by its pong. The stench of death, the buzz of flies, the indecent exposure – a stinkhorn. Rude, erect and smothered in bluebottles, the stinkhorn fungus, *Phallus impudicus*, literally 'shameless phallus', was what herbalist John Gerard called the 'prike mushroom' in 1597, and others called

Deadman's Cock. In her memoir Gwen Raverat, the engraver and granddaughter of Charles Darwin, told a story about her Aunt Hetty (Darwin's daughter) who with stick and hunting cloak collected stinkhorns from the woods and burned them in secret, reportedly to protect the morals of the maids but, given Raverat's neopagan interests, perhaps it was something more symbolic. The stinkhorn is saprobic, feeding on dead tree stumps, and its stink, which contains chemicals such as dimethyl trisulfide – associated with necrotic lesions – make the smell of carrion irresistible to blow flies. Shiny, metallic blue, green or black, the flies cluster on the green, gooey gleba that covers the cap of the fungus. The fungus disseminates itself when the gleba that contains its spores responds to the vibrations of the fly's proboscis by turning into liquid. The fly, attracted by the carrion smell, finds sugar, so instead of laying eggs on a corpse the fly is stimulated to gorge and also ingests fungal spores. Because the gleba contains protein it benefits the fly by developing eggs and the spores are transported in its faeces; their germination is unaffected by passing through a fly. Such a relationship can also involve badgers: stinkhorns are said to be more numerous around badger setts, attracting flies that will lay their eggs on dead animals; this disposes of them quickly, reducing the risk to the badger colony from disease. In warm weather, fly maggots can consume 60 per cent of a human body in less than a week. The greenwood has a macabre history of lonely deaths – suicides, murders, accidents; indifferent to tragedy, the life of woods is sustained by death, even corpses buried by robins.

A greenwood outlaw, a buzzard, perched on the high branch of a leafless tree. With its back to me, it looked out on the same scene as I did, but did we see the same thing? I saw through the trees to fields chemically enhanced with the vivid greens of new crops. The old landscape under that winter sky was a brown study: a mood induced by hedges, ash keys, muddy paths, the woods bare and misty-headed with reddish and purple-brown winter buds. The subtlety of those colours had a deepening beauty as winter thickened across the land. This buzzard was a harlequin of browns, greys and whites, and it has been suggested that because of this plumage, colour was relatively unimportant to them. I'm always impressed when I see buzzards soaring; they catch the light in the silvery feathers under their wings and their markings glow like bronze and polished wood. Such displays are for the benefit of other buzzards, not the likes of me. Perhaps because I admire these colours in the landscape, I think they're more important to the buzzard; it sees them differently, far more intensely than I do. The retina of a buzzard contains cones with five pigments (we have three) and this allows it to see far more variation in colour than I can. Without my spectacles, all this would look like muddy Impressionism, so that may be the difference between our visions.

The buzzard scanned through the landscape for traces of movement that betrayed the presence of rabbits in the wood's edge below. All ear and eye, the rabbit was as alert as an exclamation mark. It remained still and watchful, as if it thought it was invisible, when in fact its attention was so intense it seemed as obvious as a warning beacon. The young rabbit was assessing the distance of a particular threat – two people and a dog walking across a field – the distance to the burrow in the wood, an escape route across the field, the position of the other rabbits, other potential threats from land and sky. It was mapping all this through sight, sound and smell: a three, perhaps four-dimensional landscape in which an additional rabbit-sense – a prey-species instinct for survival developed over millennia – shaped its existence in the world. Around the 18th century, when people began to see the countryside as an intimate bucolic scene of picturesque beauty, rabbits were released into it – and into new Europes constructed by colonists in various parts of the world. Guns, snares, traps, dogs, disease – these were the rewards for rabbit success. Originating on the Iberian peninsula, *Oryctolagus cuniculus* – hare-like digger of underground tunnels – was domesticated by the Romans, brought to Britain by the Normans and farmed for centuries in extensive warrens. Coneys – the name for adult *rabets* – were meat for humans. Now they're free, few people eat them and all those that were persecuted as vermin for trying to take them in the past, now can. Weasels, stoats, polecats, buzzards, foxes and badgers like a bit of rabbit and many more species survive on their remains and the gardening effects of their grazing. Without them there would be even less wildlife in this sanitised, over-managed, picturesque idyll. What then is rabbit-world like? The one watching the people with a dog was already part of a complex society with hierarchies, territories, shared responsibilities and individual lives. It was taking its sentry duty seriously, protecting its community and had the makings of a dominant adult if it survived long enough. The immediate threat walked away but the rabbit could not know that another watched from far beyond the reach of its senses. What the rabbit would do in the next ten seconds would determine its fate.

A buzzard's eyes are more forward-facing than most birds; like us they have binocular vision, but unlike us they can create a telephoto optical system that detects and follows movement that to us would be a blur. Although it was searching for small mammals and birds, if hungry it may go over to the open fields to walk about picking worms and other invertebrates from the bare earth. The buzzard perched, wings folded, a beautiful grotesque, watching with an intensity of gaze that I can only guess at, deciding when to launch.

Trees stood together in companionable silence throughout a winter that leaked into a dour early spring; they fizzed with a green static as buds popped and a million leaves inflated. Hawthorns pushed their little cheesy shuttlecocks, oaks their bronze; blackthorn blossom snowed under purple dangles of ash catkins. Small birds, skirmishing through disputed branches, travelled in song between trees in the neutral air. Still for so long, life burst everywhere. Treecreepers spiralled adjacent sallows in a double helix. Chiffchaffs used the fence between wood and field to perch on before darting like children forbidden to cross a line to snatch creatures from the grass. The wren of woebetide flew from brambles across the path, letting out a burst of song loaded with omens before vanishing again. Jenny Wren is a bird of augury that belongs to an old imagination; folklore made her the wife of the robin as if they were one species – 'Robin Redbreast, Jenny Wren, God Almighty's cock and hen.' As we have already seen in Celtic mythology, the death of the wren, as Holly King for the robin as Oak King on the winter solstice, suggests sacrificial ritual from a much older time. Legend tells tales of the wren, *Troglodytes troglodytes*, as soothsayer, kept by druids in their caves for divination – 'a bird out of Merlin's ear', said Ted Hughes. This one was divining secrets discovered in her investigations of mossy holes, fulfilling her role described by Hughes as 'the inspector of the woodland's vault', sending the sharp probe of her voice through the fog of green to inspect the spirit world of the wood. A sawn stump of a storm-felled tree gathered flies, hoverflies and bees to the warmth of its honey-scented timber. Fallow deer moved through the new shadows except one; shot and wounded by a poacher it faded before it could leap the fence to greenwood sanctuary and lay dismantled by scavengers. The green carpet of dog's mercury and wild garlic filled the eye and nose grown dim with wintry grey while the embroidered violets, wood anemones, primroses, bluebells and celandines blinking in unfamiliar sunshine gladdened the heart.

In a fair season, 'blackbirds sing a full song, if there be a scanty beam of day,' in the words of an unknown Irish poet from what we now call the Dark Ages. Blackbirds, robins and others have a sub-song, an abbreviated version of their repertoire like an opera singer in rehearsal, which they perform at moments throughout the year. Where there is light, there is birdsong. Even in winter, even in the city under streetlights in the dark, robins sing. In spring, however, the birds abandon circumspection for the delirium of the 'full song'. Even the anticipation of light is enough to spark the great aural crescendo of the dawn chorus. The last 'woo-oooo' of a tawny owl meets the first clockwork hiccup of a pheasant, then bird by bird in the scanty light, the songs begin until blackbird and song thrush, willow warbler and chiffchaff, cuckoo and rook, robin and wren, all the birds sing at daybreak. Mile after mile, on one tree or many thousands, in a 'fair season' dawn sings with the collective voice of the greenwood. Some say birdsong is all sex and violence: attracting a mate, defending a territory, enticing, threatening, displaying fitness – 'come hither, come hither, come hither'. Those on the outside who hear a cacophony miss the complex beauty inside the richest aural landscape. Birds adjust the volume of their voices to background noise – weather, traffic or other birds. The early sonograms of the 1940s were the first to detect the complexity of birdsong by slowing down what we might hear as a trill or short burst of sound into separate notes arranged into a more complex phrase. Our own hearing fails to identify individual sounds when the gap between them is less than one-tenth of a second. Birds seem to have the capacity to hear in slow motion, to distinguish sounds at speeds much faster than this, detecting details lost to us. In Scottish Gaelic in 1751,

Alexander MacDonald wrote about the song thrush as a flute, 'playing its elegant piping, on the flowery tree-tops... trilling its rapid melody with quick accurate fingering.' Ornithologists such as Tim Birkhead ask, 'if we were able to hear birdsong exactly as the bird hears it, would we still consider it beautiful; would we still consider birdsong to be akin to music?' This offers delicious opportunities for speculation on the nature of music and the music of Nature. The songs of the greenwood, in the unapologetic language of rebellion, share the common beauty of the ungovernable wild.

When the light through the trees was as green and sour as a gooseberry, a high canopy of ash, latest to leaf and still sparse, allowed sunshine and showers through to lower levels aswamp with leaf, each one a crucible in the alchemy of photosynthesis, turning light into life. Dark, gnarled trunks of old hawthorns that looked so immutable all winter, had suddenly become lithe and sinuous like shadow dancers behind curtains of hazel, on carpets of dog's mercury, in chambers full of birdsong. When the sun was out, the birds drawled softly in the heady air; when it rained they held their breaths; when the rain stopped and the woodland labyrinths were rinsed clean, they released their voices, cool and sweet. The woods were steeped in rhythm: light and shade, breath and wing, movement and stillness – all these languages tell commonplace, ordinary, everyday stories of living woods but in spring it felt so recklessly giddy. It was easy to conjure the Puck of 'Mad Pranks and Merry Jest', Lincoln green outlaws carolling in their cups, a choir of birds chanting endorphin levels up in their brains.

The moments of transition between seasons are swift. Spring is often an all-at-once happening and all at once it will be gone. Its green dazzle masks an absence. There are not enough birds, not enough butterflies. Perhaps this throws the individual, the particular, into relief and gives it greater significance. A speckled wood butterfly flickering through dappled shade becomes clearer in focus but where are all the other missing butterflies and moths? Did they dissolve in this vanishing green to become memories like old leaves rotted in woodland mulch? Questions hover like gnats in a 'scanty beam of day' and vanish. Birds forage and pause for a moment before singing again and then the woods give voice. Under the greenwood tree, our voices and those of birds become one song of sanctuary with, 'No enemy/But winter and rough weather.' We feel it still, and we also know how easily it could all be lost by our own doing; it is we who will stand accused in the archetypal poem, 'Who Killed Cock Robbin?'.

> *All the birds of the air*
> *Fell to sighing and sobbing*
> *When they heard the bell toll*
> *For poor Cock Robbin.*

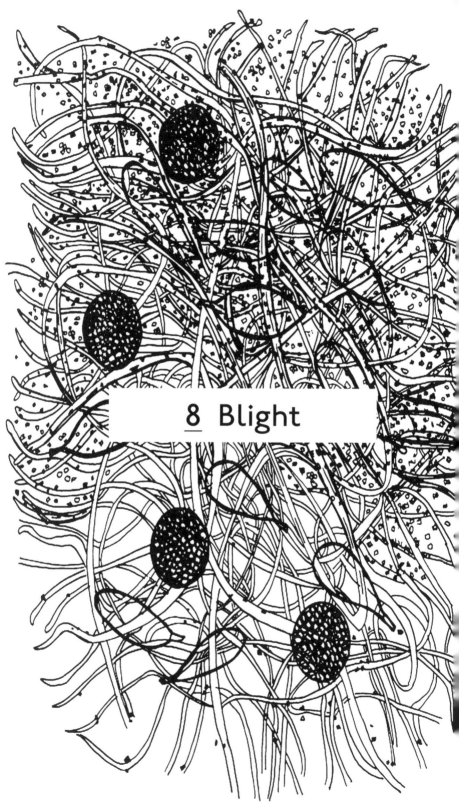

8 Blight

I WALKED PAST THE TREE almost every day for over ten years, a common lime tree, *Tilia* × *europaea*, planted perhaps 100 years ago as part of a row between the lane and the field, possibly as a commemorative planting or a way of creating an avenue to the entrance of the medieval ruins of Wenlock Priory. I began to notice that this particular tree, located at the end of the row closest to the stream, was looking sickly, its crown thinning, its trunk oozing with sticky black lesions. There were no fungal fruiting bodies present, but the tree was obviously infected, and after a couple of years of decline it was cut down. I had seen this kind of effect before on chestnut trees and oaks and was sure the pathogen was a *Phytophthora*, its Greek scientific name meaning, 'plant destroyer'. The dying tree was a loss, to the wildlife that lived in it and to those, like me, who were fond of it. I was not the only one sad to see such a vibrant, healthy, classically beautiful tree deteriorate like an old friend suffering. It was tempting to medicalise the tree's condition as a disease, a sickness that could spread to infect other trees, something that should be treated, perhaps even cured. The blighted lime tree was also a reminder that trees are communities of different organisms, such as symbiotic mycorrhizal fungi that sustain them, parasitic fungi that feed on them and saprophytic fungi that recycle them when they die. If we expect a balance in this community to last for centuries, then an organism that confronts the healthy, timber tree archetype by killing its host becomes a dark agent of destruction. I'm not sure it is right to see the blight of *Phytophthora* and other pathogens in this light. They are fascinating, complicated organisms, many of them are new here and the destruction they cause is largely our responsibility.

Phytophthora are neither plants, animals nor fungi, but protists, eukaryotic (having nuclei) microorganisms that are diploid – with pairs of chromosomes – and cellulose, with cell walls like plants, but producing oospores without sexual reproduction and zoospores with it; they grow filaments of mycelium like fungi and are pathogens, living parasitically on plants. The spores travel through water to reach the fine roots of trees or the root collar where they form filaments that feed on the cells and rot them; they may travel in the cambium and phloem of the inner bark to girdle the tree's trunk, choking the life out of it. Currently *Phytophthora* are called oomycetes – water moulds. The most infamous of these being *Phytophthora infestans*, the late potato blight that caused the 19th-century Irish Famine.

The potato was grown by Incas in the Andes mountains and brought to Europe by Spanish seafarers where, related to deadly nightshade, it was treated with caution at first. Once a delicacy fit for a Queen, by 1629 it had become commonplace, and by 1800 was becoming a staple diet, particularly for the poor. The potato was grown extensively in Ireland where the climate and soils were ideal for potato growing, but the land and trade was entirely controlled by the English. During the cold, wet weather of 1845, potato leaves began to show signs of infection and withered. The following year the blight spores, using their flagella to swim through sodden fields, increased exponentially and Ireland's potato crop turned to sludge. Between 1846 and 1860, one million people died of starvation, and 1.5 million emigrated, leaving a population that has still not recovered over 170 years later, and a legacy of resentment against the English who could have prevented it. The potato blight had developed a mating type to produce zoospores and became even more difficult to control.

Blight is a story of pathogens introduced into ecosystems that have no resistance to them. The sudden loss of British elm trees is a stark reminder of this in modern times. Elm tree disease fungus, *Ceratocystis ulmi*, carried by the elm bark beetle, came to Britain from Europe around 4000BCE and so was part of the woodland ecosystem. The fungus was taken to North America in the 1920s where it destroyed millions of American elms and went through a genetic alteration. When the fungus returned to Europe, it had changed into a much more virulent form to become *Ophiostoma (Ceratocystis) novo-ulmi*, the Dutch Elm Disease that struck Britain in the 1970s and wiped out most mature elms. I remember felling dead elms at that time, and seeing in the occasional blackened annual rings of old trees that they had suffered from an elm disease fungal infection in the past but had survived, whereas the new form had killed them. Elms had been resistant to the fungus for millennia but had no resistance to the new strain of the same species that emerged from North America. The loss, within a decade, of so many individual trees that had defined the character of the landscape was shocking. Apart from the pockets of elms that escaped the disease in parts of Scotland, East Anglia, East Sussex and the Scilly Isles. English elm, *Ulmus procera*, smooth-leaved elm, *U. carpinifolia* and wych elm, *U. glabra* hang on as suckers from the roots of felled trees in hedgerows or field corners, but usually succumb to the disease when they begin to mature; they hold the hope that eventually elms will develop a resistance to *Ophiostoma novo-ulmi*. Dreadful as Dutch Elm Disease was, the threat of blight to ash and oak trees would be devastating and it is now a growing possibility.

Different species of water moulds are found across the world and have been around for a long time as pathogens of plant crops and trees. Human traffic and the trade in forest products and plants for nurseries and garden centres in Europe, Asia, Africa and the Americas has increased the global distribution of these pathogens, enabling them to spread in different forms, make use of new hosts and evolve hybrids between species previously separated on different continents. The water mould, *Phytophthora cinnamomi,* believed to have come from Papua New Guinea, arrived in western Australia in the early 20th century and as 'jarra dieback' devastated forests there; it killed holm and cork oaks in southern Europe and is implicated in the decline of oaks from Britain to Romania since the 1920s; *P. cinnamomi* now affects thousands of plant species and often exists in conjunction with other water-mould species in the same hosts.

In the mid-1990s, a pathogen came to the world's attention in the San Francisco Bay and southern Oregon areas of the USA. Oaks, maples, azaleas, laurels, chestnuts and other trees were found suffering from oozing cankers and many died suddenly. Identified as *Phytophthora ramorum*, the water mould was dubbed Sudden Oak Death. Around 2002, plants with leaf blemishes and dying stems started appearing in British nurseries and garden centres. The water mould causing this was also found to be *P. ramorum.* Diseased plants were destroyed by officials from the Department for Environment, Food and Rural Affairs (Defra), but the British version of Sudden Oak Death was different to the American one. It jumped the garden centre fence and appeared in some mature trees but then moved into *Rhododendron ponticum,* the naturalised rhododendron and from there, by 2011, into larch plantations. Since then, it has wiped out Japanese larch in much of the west of England and Wales. Britain's native oaks belong to a range that, as yet, have been resistant to

P. ramorum. The situation is complicated by there being several different strains of this particular water mould and confusion about its origins, which seem to involve native forms coming into contact with repeatedly introduced forms from America, Europe and perhaps Asia – it has been discovered in Vietnam – and it is very dynamic. Transmitted by both airborne and waterborne spores, cultivated unwittingly by gardeners, *P. ramorum* has two different lifestyles. It infects some trees with stem cankers and kills them, and in other plants it infects leaves and shoots but is not fatal. The American form has a wide range of species involved in its disease cycle. One of the strains may involve a mating type from rhododendron centres of diversity in China or the Himalayas, and it prefers a warm, Mediterranean-type climate. So far, there are at least four identified forms of *P. ramorum* in America and Europe. The spread of fungal and water-mould pathogens has a lot to do with changes in traditional cultivation methods and the distribution of spores through the movement of infected soils and living material in international trade.

There is also a climatic influence in the expansion of blights. Stress in trees as a result of droughts and unseasonable late rains has benefited many water moulds. In Europe, *P. cinnamomi* is most pathogenic at 25°C (77°F) or above and does not survive freezing. Computer models for climate change – assuming a 1.5°–3°C (2.7–5.4°F) increase over the next 100 years – predict that the pathogens will expand massively as climate change and habitat disturbance increase. This will favour many water moulds with disastrous implications for forests, woodlands and the wildlife that depend on them. During the 20th century there were around 54 water-mould species recorded; in less than two decades since then the number may be anything from 200–600. If the general assumption that only 10 per cent of fungi species have been discovered so far, then that number is set to increase dramatically.

Just when the ecological, social and economic benefits of planting native trees to mop up the effects of climate-change-related flooding have been recognised, another water mould emerged killing the alder trees of riverside and wetland habitats. The alder water mould, *Phytophthora alni*, may be a hybrid organism in which neither of the parent species is thought to be native to Europe, and was probably introduced through the trade in plants or plant products. Established in river systems since 1993 in southern England, the Midlands and Scotland, *P. alni* produces weeping cankers in alders, which usually prove fatal but may be managed by coppicing. It has spread to Ireland, Austria, Belgium, Germany, Hungary, Italy, Lithuania, Holland and Sweden, and appears to have got into trees grown mainly in German and Dutch nurseries for planting in Europe and, irrigated by river water, has quickly spread throughout river catchments. Since spores are waterborne, trees infect rivers and rivers infect trees. In many British river systems, half the alder trees are affected.

Of the water moulds currently active in Britain, *Phytophthora austrocedri* appeared in Teesdale in the North Pennines in 2011 as dieback in native juniper and came from Patagonia. *P. kernoviae* was first found in Cornwall in 2003, and is now in Britain, Ireland and New Zealand damaging beech trees and native oaks. *P. lateralis* kills Lawson cypress in western Oregon and north-west California and arrived in Britain in 2010 where Lawson cypress hybrids and horticultural forms are some of the most popular trees in gardens. *P. quercina* causes yellowing of leaves, crown dieback and root rot in native oak species, as does *P. cambivora*, another introduced species.

Until the 1970s, most nurseries propagated their own shrubs from stock plants and this limited the exposure to new diseases. Since then, cheaper plant material has flooded in from around the world, and the pathogens have hitched a ride. Back in the USA, where Sudden Oak Death is spreading rapidly in the forests of the Pacific North-West, new species, including redwood and Douglas fir, are believed to be at risk. The concern is that because the disease affects so many forest species, it could prove worse than the American chestnut blight that appeared at New York's Bronx Zoo in 1904, and spread so rapidly that within 40 years it virtually wiped out the eastern species of American chestnut – about four billion trees. Like many blights, this was assumed to have come from the East in nursery plants or plant products. While there are biosecurity codes of practice for tree growers and some restrictions of movement, fungicides do not solve the problem, only masking the effect of the fungi. As the research continues, water moulds are rapidly adapting and spreading around the world with dazzling success. This biological dynamic plus trees grown in one country where a blight becomes active and planted in another without sufficient biosecurity controls, is the story behind ash disease.

In 2009, some horticulturalists were concerned about a disease in ash trees and a survey revealed the presence of a protist fungi that is two entities in one. During summer, *Chalara fraxinea* is the pathogenic stage infecting ash leaves and stems, producing a poison called viridiol that causes black spots and wilting of leaves, and bruising and cankers on stems; then a mass of gooey spores that spread around the tree via rain causes further infections. In autumn, *Chalara* turns into *Hymenoscyphus pseudoalbidus*, so-called because it was originally thought to be a fungus called *Hymenoscyphus albidus* that lived on dead ash leaves, but subsequently turned out to be something new that could have come to Europe from China or Japan, or could be a hybrid. It forms little white cups on the separated midribs of fallen leaves, each cup puffing out over a thousand windblown spores to infect other trees. When the ash leaves open, the *Hymenoscyphus* fungus reverts to *Chalara* and repeats its lifecycle. Because of the genetic diversity of ash, many trees die, some become infected several times and others manage to survive ash disease. Ash trees imported from Europe to plant in native woodland planting schemes throughout the UK have spread *Chalara* extensively. There is no controlling it from these plantings or from windborne spores blown across the North Sea or stuck to boots or birds' feet; 2012 was the worst year for infections so far and there is no pattern as yet to make a prediction on the future of ash trees in Britain. However, as the historical ecologist Oliver Rackham warned, the main threat to ash now comes from 'one of the most feared beetles on Earth', the emerald ash borer, that has not yet arrived in Britain but is ominously closing in.

The global horticulture market and government regulators cannot cope with the dynamics of pathogens such as *Chalara* and *Phytophthora*. They are spreading too quickly and with frightening ecological consequences for woodland and forest collapse. Each tree belongs to an ecosystem and is one in itself; this makes the loss of each tree significant. The lime tree I watched sicken and die before it was felled was quickly followed in the same field by two old horse chestnut trees that succumbed, probably, to *P. cinnamomi*, and were also cut down. I live surrounded by ash woods. The elms went 40 years ago; so far, ash disease has not had a huge impact locally but that may change.

Fungi, including oomycetes, account for 30 per cent of the emerging diseases in plants. Of these, between 65 and 85 per cent of plant pathogens are alien to the location of their host plants. For all their devastating effects, pathogens such as water moulds are delicate, ephemeral entities that are really a biological response to our globalisation, climate change and the commodification of Nature. They are the ecology of the Anthropocene. We see them as destroyers of things we love or need but, although it often feels otherwise, Nature is savagely and beautifully indifferent to our preferences. When we set about protecting the Nature we like from the Nature we don't like, we impose human values on wild processes with no idea what the long-term effect will be. In imposing our will on the planet, the planet has responded with something very different to our intentions. Pathogens are as much a part of Nature as the trees they infect and the wildlife that coexists with them. The fascinating, yet frightening blights are just organisms whose astounding diversity and adaptability has been enhanced by human ecological disturbance. We may not like this kind of biodiversity, but it is going to shape civilisation and the ecology of the world.

9 The Returned

ONE SUMMER EVENING, two years ago, I thought I saw a pine marten. Leaving a wood at dusk on Wenlock Edge, we both crossed the lane together. I saw a chocolate brown, cat-like creature, low and swift, run across the lane and vanish into a hedge. By the time I got through a gate into the field to arrive at the other side of the point I had seen the animal disappear, it was long gone, or else it was watching me and I couldn't see it. Although I told myself the animal I'd seen was probably a polecat, I very much wanted to confirm rumours that pine martens were about; I couldn't prove my sighting. I just had a feeling.

One of Britain's rarest and most elusive mammals, pine martens were thought to be extinct in England and Wales and restricted to parts of Scotland, until a report of few years ago revealed they had been living a secret life under our noses for decades. Pine martens, *Martes martes*, are mustelids, related to weasels and otters; they are agile, inquisitive and about the size of a large ferret or small cat. With deep chestnut fur and a diagnostic yellow bib, the 80cm (31½in) of apex predator between beady black nose and bushy tail tip is a supreme hunter of voles, rabbits, hares, squirrels, birds and their eggs; they also eat honey, nuts, fruit and fungi. Beautiful fur and a killer instinct, particularly when it came to game birds, made pine martens both valuable and vermin, persecuted to extinction in most parts of Britain. Even with full legal protection in 1988, only small enclaves hung on in remote parts of northern Scotland, Cumbria and North Wales. Or so it was thought.

A few years ago, a Vincent Wildlife Trust report based on 12 years of research and sightings, revealed a surprise: pine martens were still present in broadly the same parts of England and Wales from which they were recorded in the past. This included areas such as Carmarthenshire, Montgomery, the North York Moors and the Cheviots, but also odd sightings in Cambridge, East Sussex and Northampton. In 2010, conservationists were ecstatic to report the finding of pine marten scat in the Cheviot Hills of Northumberland. After 50 reported sightings there since the mid-1990s this casual defecation was described as the 'holy grail' for those searching for the elusive martens of England. An extensive search was organised from Northumberland to Cumbria but the martens remained hidden.

The presence of mythical martens in the English countryside was beginning to sound like big-cat stories. For decades there had been sightings of animals described as pumas, panthers and lynx at large in the British countryside. I have personally interviewed people who have seen big, usually black, cats and others who are hunting them for proof of their existence. My impression of the people I've met who have reported sightings or claim to have seen big cats and not reported them because they wanted to avoid media attention and accusations of being cranks or deluded simpletons, is that they honestly think they've seen these animals, are intelligent and know the difference between large dogs and big cats. I can't be sure but I think I once saw a big black cat in the woods above my house, but then I also wanted to make what I saw crossing the road into a pine marten. Despite what big-cat specialists say about the ability of leopards and others to hide in plain sight, in Britain with such a tradition of wildlife observation, how could an animal, even a nocturnal, arboreal one as large as a pine marten, pass unnoticed for so long? Some dedicated naturalists, who had been watching them for many years, hoped the species' presence would eventually be recognised. The trouble was that cheap and easy survey methods did not work on something as elusive and scarce as pine martens; the perception had arisen that there were none left. From 1996–2007, researchers analysed records, talked to people with convincing sightings, collected roadkill and tested the DNA of scat, slowly piecing together a picture of a creature so hard to pin down, few believed it existed at all and taking comfort from the astrophysicists' mantra: 'an absence of evidence is not an evidence of absence'. English sightings had been dismissed as feral cats, polecats, mink or even black squirrels. Others have been explained as escapees from wildlife centres. This annoyed those who were perfectly capable of identifying a pine marten when they saw one and confused people like me who thought they might have seen one but didn't trust themselves. For pine martens to pass from legend required proof.

The observations of amateur naturalists are key but there are fewer people dedicated to carefully engaged observation, honing their fieldcraft and building up their skills in the hope of making a discovery. Such naturalists are an endangered species. Birding in the Shropshire Hills, Dave Pearce saw a pine marten running through the wood and sent two photographs of it to the Shropshire Wildlife Trust. Meticulous verification was accepted by the Vincent Wildlife Trust as scientifically valid and an animal that was thought to be extinct in England for a century turned out to have returned but may in fact have been there for a long time.

Pine martens can easily travel 20km (12½ miles) in a day overland and their specially adapted furry feet enable them to move overhead through trees. They are highly territorial, with adults pushing out younger, smaller ones to find new territories of their own. It is very likely the Shropshire marten had come from Wales as a pioneer seeking new territory. Like the polecat, buzzard and raven, the presence of pine martens in England is not thought to depend on escapes from zoos, fur farms, private collections or from deliberate reintroductions, but to the fact that they have been hanging on in spite of us. Their resilience is a lesson in the ability of some species to keep a population ticking over, waiting for the opportunity to expand and take advantage of changes in land use and management. The pine martens are benefiting from changing woodland and forestry practices, fewer of them being killed, more woodland being planted for carbon offsetting and amenity purposes.

The presence of pine martens is certainly something to celebrate and there are movements afoot to reintroduce them to many parts of Britain where they were thought to have been persecuted to extinction. But maybe the Shropshire marten suggests that leaving animals to find their own way back may be a better policy than kidnapping them from the wild and releasing them into territories they have no connection with and that may well be the territories of existing pine martens not yet discovered. The future of these charming, deadly and graceful animals with great intelligence depends on how woodlands matter to society. Creating new woodland, protecting old ones, particularly those trees with breeding holes in them and championing greater connectivity between woodlands will allow pine martens to stay away from predatory foxes and regain their rightful place in the trees. They are totem animals of the greenwood, symbols of resistance, and just the knowledge they exist, even if we can't see them hiding in the shadows, is a wild hope to hang on to.

The newsworthiness of exotic creatures, such as panthers, pumas, wolverines and racoon dogs roaming Britain's

shadowlands, has lessened since the beginning of the century.
However, real or not, such reported sightings may have
changed the public perception of big cats in the countryside,
making them more rather than less acceptable. There was
public outrage when a young lynx that escaped from Borth
Zoo in Wales was shot by the council in 2017. Local farmers
were concerned for their sheep, the local authority felt it had
a duty to protect the public, but many people were hoping an
animal so ruthlessly exterminated from Britain may return, as

it had in other parts of Europe. The idea that lynx could return to Britain has been argued by conservationists and supporters of rewilding for many years now. The Eurasian lynx, *Lynx lynx* is a secretive, powerful cat with tufted ears and short tail weighing 25kg (55lb) that hung on in Britain until c.180CE. The lynx is a much more likely mammal predator candidate for reintroduction than the wolf. Given sightings and occasional reports, it may already have been released here, I was told by hunting interests. Not so fussy about habitat requirements, it is estimated that the Scottish Highlands could support a population of 400 lynx where they would keep down roe-deer numbers as well as foxes.

It is always a possibility that when confronted with a tradition of intractable prejudice, the only way many animals wiped out from Britain will return is through illegal or accidental releases. Wild boar, *Sus scrofa*, after an absence of 400 years, have reintroduced themselves by escaping from boar farms damaged by the 1987 storm. There are now populations in south-east and south-west England and the Forest of Dean. The recent history of beavers in Britain, on the other hand, is a mixture of planned and unplanned reintroduction and some escapes. Hunted to extinction for their fur and scent glands in the 12th century in England, and extinct in Britain since the 16th century, it was not until three escaped from a study colony in Devon a couple of years ago that a wild beaver, *Castor fiber*, swam free in an English river. Their freedom may have been short-lived but thanks to reintroductions there are 20 or 30 beavers here. Ecologists have been showing how beavers are the main change agents for the restoration of river catchments. Their dam building and coppicing streamside trees conserve water in the landscape and hugely increase biodiversity in many studies. When governments eventually believe this is more important than the damaging agricultural and development interests that are doing the opposite, beavers will return. Unlike some parts of Europe where beavers have been reintroduced by being thrown out of the back of a van, here in the UK the return of once extinct wild animals to the British countryside is treated with Kafkaesque feasibility studies, public consultations, legal wrangling, interminable arguments, fierce opposition from landowning interests and meticulous planning. It took from 1994, when beaver reintroduction to Scotland was proposed, to 2009 for animals to be released in Knapdale after an absence of 400 years. Others have joined them unofficially. Even though beavers now have native-species status in Scotland and their populations, about 250 so far, are being allowed to expand naturally through river systems, many are being shot by landowners.

The tortuous process of reintroducing species into the wild in Britain depends on trust between landowners and conservationists to manage them and their habitats effectively. Studies are underway; ecologists are showing water companies how beavers help water filtration, removing pollutants and conserving water supply to reservoirs. Beavers are described as ecosystem engineers, bringing real environmental benefits, and it is the argument about Nature as capital, resource and provider of ecosystem services to people, that is supposed to sell the idea of reintroduction and persuade landowners. It is an argument with even bigger ambitions. Reports by scientists from UK, Norway and other European countries in support of wolf reintroduction in Scotland look at the effect of wolves on Scotland's deer population by simulating what has happened elsewhere. The last wolf, *Canis lupus*, was killed in Scotland in the 17th century. According to recent population modelling, if wolves were reintroduced to Scotland their population would stabilise at 25 wolves per 1,000sq. km (386 sq. miles). Although this would have an effect on extremely high red deer population, experience in other countries shows the wider effect would be to regenerate vegetation and woodland, benefiting wildlife and helping to restore ecosystems. The reintroduction of wolves into America's Yellowstone National Park gave rise to the theory of trophic cascades: the ecological effects of the introduced predator on reducing the population and increasing the fitness of grazing animals, the release of grazing pressure on the vegetation and the effect this had on wider species diversity, erosion, water quality and so on throughout the ecosystem, was the reverse of previous restoration theories that tried to re-create an ecosystem and add the apex predator at the end. The long-standing debate on wolf reintroduction had been largely driven by anecdote and fear. Scientists can now use the trophic cascades approach to wolf reintroduction to Britain to show how its ecological effects can transform the whole ecosystem. Those who argue that reintroductions need grassroots support and cannot succeed as impositions by authorities but only as a public response to what society wants from open spaces, say the choice is between intensive agriculture or diverse ecosystems, tourism, water quality and other ecosystem services. The reintroduction of the white-tailed eagle on the Scottish island of Mull, for example, is a popular example that has developed an industry around wildlife watching. In 1700 there were 200 pairs of white-tailed eagle, *Haliaeetus albicilla*, but by 1916 this huge bird, sometimes called the sea eagle, became extinct through illegal persecution in the UK. It was reintroduced to Scotland from Scandinavia in 1975 and although successful, even after 40 years there are only 40 or so breeding pairs in Britain and they are vulnerable to power cables, Highland wildfires and illegal poisoning. Proposals to reintroduce them to other parts of their British range, such as East Anglia, are embroiled in local-interest arguments.

It is assumed that British people have to see the benefits of rewilded landscapes, to balance the benefits of a productive countryside with wildlife for recreation and tourism that contribute to ecosystem services. Alladale Wilderness Reserve in the Scottish Highlands, Knepp Castle in West Sussex and a host of new rewilding projects around Britain are attempting to prove that landscape-scale ecological restoration through reintroducing missing species to the ecosystem and allowing Nature to manage as far as animal welfare legislation will go, are compatible with modern British life. These projects were inspired by the pioneering work of ecologist Frans Vera at Oostvaardersplassen in Holland, a 5,000ha (1,236 acre) reserve reclaimed from the sea in 1968, internationally important for migrating wildfowl and managed by roaming herds of red deer, Konik ponies and Heck cattle. Adventurous conservationists claim such large nature reserves need not be compartmentalised as they are in Holland, with sharp edges defining productive and wild land. A realism about our dependency on air, soil and water and more enlightened policies applied to different landscapes and subsidies, could go hand in hand with the reintroductions of grazers and predators missing from landscapes to restore habitats.

The current reintroductions and many of the candidates for future reintroductions do not require landscape-scale ecological restoration for their success. For example, because of successful reintroductions, the red kite, *Milvus milvus*, now has the highest population for 200 years in the UK, with 2,000 breeding pairs. A bird so common in Shakespearean times that they stole food from children and handkerchiefs from ladies in the streets of London was, by the later 20th century, restricted to a small area in West Wales. In her poem about feeding them with offal, 'Red Kites at Tregaron', Gwyneth Lewis wrote, 'What is most foul/in me kites love. At night I feel/their clear minds stirring in rowan and oak/out in the desert.' Persecution from farmers and gamekeepers and egg collecting had made the red kite almost extinct in Britain, but reintroductions of birds of Swedish and Spanish origin between 1989 and 2004 have made their floating, coppery, chevrons a common sight along roads from the Chilterns to Gateshead to Aberdeen. White-tailed eagles too can float over the existing landscape without its modification. Great bustards favour the Ministry of Defence grassland and arable fields on Salisbury Plain. In 2007, the first egg for 175 years of a great bustard, *Otis tarda*, was laid in Britain by introduced birds. Hunted to extinction, this emblem of Wiltshire and the heaviest flying bird in the world, weighing up to 20kg (44lb), was reintroduced to Salisbury Plain. The project began in 2004 with eggs rescued from farmland in Russia and raised to release in the UK a few at a time. Great bustards need open grassland and arable fields where they feed on grasshoppers and cereal seeds.

Not all reintroduced species are so enormous; some become iconic and candidates for reintroduction because of their importance to the naturalists who study them and for their aesthetic value. The large blue butterfly, *Maculinea arion*, is one of the most vulnerable butterflies in the world. It lays its eggs on wild thyme and then the caterpillars are adopted by red ants, who take them into their nests where the butterfly caterpillars become predators of ant grubs, before pupating and emerging as spectacularly bright blue adults. Extinct in the UK in 1975 the large blue was reintroduced to Dartmoor in 2000 from Sweden. However, even the most iconic candidates for reintroduction could also arrive without any restoration: lynx seem happy to live in existing broadleaved woodland or conifer plantations.

Facing a list of 1,149 priority wildlife species and 65 priority habitats which require concerted action to save

them from disappearing, the government's chances of fulfilling
its commitment to stop the loss of biodiversity before 2020 is
unlikely. The reintroduction of charismatic fauna as emblems
of wildness offers conservation bodies opportunities to
engage with the public in ways that obscure species of plants
and invertebrates in isolated nature reserves do not. Many
environmentalists believe there is a moral imperative to correct
anthropogenic harm and a moral obligation to maintain
habitats and improve them from damage caused by agriculture.
Some argue that, as well as environmental justice, we need the
returned for our own spiritual wellbeing. Ecologist and author,
Peter Taylor, says, 'the reintroduction of charismatic species is
also a way of rewilding the human mind, creating excitement,
breaking out of the ghetto of conservation viewed as stamp
collecting, and engaging people with Nature on a deeper
psychological level.'

Every return of an animal or plant puts something back.
It's an ecological promise for the future. The deliberate
reintroductions of beavers, red kites or large blue butterflies
each strike against a nihilism that casts Nature as a patient
in terminal decline. But what we have to remember is that
these are wild creatures, not just symbols or tokens that can
be brought back to right historical wrongs. Like the pine
marten, the most successful returns are those which have
avoided human agency. In the wood I wandered in, just
before I thought I saw a pine marten, I had been watching
and listening to the most successful and darkest revenant of
centuries of slaughter.

A raven called from above the wood and another answered.
My gaze followed their flight westwards into the Welsh
Marches, a landscape with a violent history epitomised
by the poet A.E. Housman: 'There the ravens feasted far/
About the open house of war.' Housman lamented the role

his ancestors and mine played in wars between Saxon and Celt across the border and their tragic legacy that remained hidden in this countryside. The call of birds, whose ancestors once stole the eyes of our ancestors who fell in battle, rang through the sky. In the 19th-century rise of the hunting estates, gamekeepers who were zealously protecting grouse and pheasants and shepherds who were protecting lambs and injured ewes, trapped, shot and poisoned ravens with baited carcasses – a practice that continues today on some estates. Relentless persecution drove them back to the fastness of the west – Wales, Cornwall, Cumbria and the Scottish Islands. With a morbid irony, the first step in the raven's return began on the battlefields of Europe during the First World War, when so many gamekeepers and shepherds were killed. The pattern of employment in the British countryside was never the same and the Second World War had a similar effect. Reduced persecution and more open land for colonisation, led to the gradual expansion of raven territory. During the 1980s, gamekeeping practices changed; chicks were reared in hatcheries before release, making ravens less of a threat. In the hills, EU headage payments increased the number of sheep and therefore the mortality rate, which greatly benefited the raven population. Before BSE disease, farmers would sell dead sheep to the knacker's yard or the local hunt but because of a panic about food-chain contamination, carcasses were required to be buried – not an easy operation in the uplands.

Ravens are the most efficient undertakers. They watch people, as they watch wolves, in the knowledge that observation will be rewarded with the opportunity of a death. Perhaps this is why ravens are the most written about, most storied and mythologised bird across the northern hemisphere. Ravens are in the hills because that is where the sheep are, and although they like rocky places, including cathedrals, they nest in big trees or even telecommunications masts and can adapt anywhere they can keep a weather eye on the way people and death rub up together. Adult ravens begin breeding at four or five years of age; before that they are gregarious. Breeding pairs move away to establish their own territories which they fiercely defend. The spectacular population boom of recent decades will depend on agricultural changes and competition from red kites and buzzards. The pair I see appear strong and confident, they have returned to reclaim their lands as if fulfilling an ancient prophecy. Perhaps ravens can see the future.

10 A Bestiary

IN THE MIDDLE AGES, a bestiary was a gazette of natural history and folklore about creatures real, imaginary, speculative and mythological, often containing moral instruction based on the way the animals represented aspects of human behaviour and were symbolic of religious notions. These cultural ways of seeing Nature linked animals to the ecology of creation in the medieval imagination, in which relations between people and animals were framed by the controlling powers of state and church and their wars between good and evil, virtue and sin, civilisation and wildness. Since Darwin, we have come to see Nature in terms of organic systems made up of individuals in cooperation or competition, similar to the way we see society, politics and economics. Advances in technology, e.g. microscopy, photography, DNA sequencing and satellite imaging, have radically improved the life sciences but how we see Nature depends on what we see it with. Technology frames how we think about Nature and how we think shapes the technology we need to reveal further mysteries. The more we look, the more we see, but what are we examiners really searching for, if not ourselves? What we now understand about the interrelationship and interdependence of things, the revelation that all of us – people, foxes, jellyfish – are evolving, dynamic, communities of cells, is changing how we see our relationships with Nature. Something of the medieval imagination, and a more ancient animism it tried to replace, roams the margins where the limitations of technology meet our feelings for creatures in the stories we tell about them. This is an alphabetical bestiary of British wildlife, idiosyncratic in its selection and based on personal encounter.

ADDER, northern or common European viper, *Vipera berus*

Double Diamond was trying to absorb the sunlight of a dull summer morning in the Wyre Forest of Worcestershire. She detected the scent of the old adversary through a flick of her forked tongue. Adders are 'deaf', the vertical slits in their pupils detect movement but they largely perceive the world through their tongues, so they hear as well as smell and taste through them. Gracefully fluid, she uncoiled into the tangle of shadows and vanished. Double Diamond, according to Sylvia Sheldon, the adder lady of Wyre Forest, is 61 cm (24in) long, 16-and-a-half years old, had recently shed her skin and was pregnant. She would go to a favourite place to give birth in September to seven or eight babies, which she would incubate inside her. Sylvia knew the adders as individuals. Her photographs revealed each had markings on their heads as unique as fingerprints and she used these curious inverted

'V', 'A' and chess piece-shaped glyphs to identify them. Male adders grow up to 60cm (23½in) long and 60g (just over 2oz) in weight; they are white to grey with a distinctive inverted 'V' on their heads and the diagnostic black zigzag along their spines; they have ritual contests of strength called the Dance of the Adders. Females are larger than males, up to 75cm (29½in) long and 100g (3½oz) in weight, usually brown with a dark head and zigzag markings; they give birth to live offspring in special antenatal places out of sight. Adders are the only snakes found inside the Arctic Circle. They are said to live for 20 years but one of Sylvia's adders is 32. Adders are most commonly seen in March and April after they've emerged from winter hideaways – hibernacula (underground burrows or tunnels) – and on summer and early autumn days when it's cooler and they need to bask to warm up. They prefer woodland edges, heathland and rough grassland on sandy soils. Although localised and scarce in many places, they are distributed throughout the UK and can be seen on Surrey Heaths, the Gower Peninsula, Wyre Forest, North York Moors, the Scottish Highlands and the Shetland Islands. Adders only bite in self-defence. There are about 100 cases of adder bites each year, but few are ever serious; if bitten, seek medical attention as they can cause swelling, nausea and faintness. Because adders are venomous, people are frightened of them but, as Sylvia points out, they are not aggressive: they're beautiful, timid and only want to get as far away from people as possible. They eat mice and voles and never attack people, only biting those who try to grab them. However, the old prejudices that led to the persecution of vipers still linger in the countryside and hibernacula are vulnerable to destruction by vehicles. Adders are protected by law and it is illegal to handle or injure them.

BADGER, European badger, *Meles meles*

A few miles north of where I live in Shropshire, the bodies
of two badgers were X-rayed and found to have been shot
before they were dumped on the roadside. Badgers have
become political animals and the assassinations of those
two confirmed a long-standing rural myth that badgers are
slaughtered illegally and made to look like roadkill. In some
areas, badgers are said to be extinct because of this ecological
cleansing. For all its current standing as a protected species
and an emblem of conservation, the badger has been the victim
of human aggression for centuries. However this violence has
been meted out – whether baited with dogs for sport, shot
or gassed for trespass and fear of disease – the indigenous
badger is also admired for its qualities of resilience, fortitude
and independence, and its victimhood marks a kind of
cultural ownership. John Clare wrote of the badger's bravery
and fortitude when baited by dogs and villagers, 'He turns
about to face the loud uproar/And drives the rebels to their
very door.' Although violence against wildlife may appear
to be old-fashioned prejudice dressed up in business and
sporting interests, something else is going on as well. Bovine
tuberculosis, for instance, has propelled an old prejudice to the
fore. Since achieving legal protection, the badger population
in Britain has increased to unprecedented levels. Some see this
as a damaging overpopulation, while others claim it's a natural
response to reduced persecution; but what is happening in
agriculture, where the theory has taken hold that TB in cattle
will be treated by killing badgers, is a reassertion of the feudal
ownership of wild Nature. Those supporting a bearing down
on wildlife believe they have every right to do so – this is their
land, their wildlife. Such people see this right being opposed
by sentimental townies who simply don't understand the
realities of the countryside. However, political manoeuvrings

to weaken or remove those environmental protection laws that may impede business interests are increasing. It's clear too that a badger cull – badgers are protected by UK and EU legislation – was also intended to test these laws, making the statutory body responsible for protecting wildlife the same as the licensing authority that sanctions its slaughter. Public opinion opposed to the badger cull will further convince a rural minority that they are the victims in all this. Still smarting from the ban on fox hunting, still suffering from ever-depleting services and a repopulation by incomers with different values, sections of rural society are using wildlife as scapegoats for their frustrations and resentments. Wildlife, loved by the majority, has in some parts of Britain become symbolic of the interests of an elite and aroused a culture of cruelty and of transferring historical resentment back onto 'vermin'. This will not be solved by a few criminal convictions for killing badgers, if there ever are any, and talk of education, but by standing up for Nature and dealing with the relics of feudalism, social inequalities and opportunities for rural communities.

CROW, carrion crow, *Corvus corone*

There is a nervousness about the crow's swagger, as if it's concentrating on something else, nothing to do with an egg – never noticed it before. Then it half-hops, half-shimmies a few steps towards it. Head cocked, one eye over its wing to see who else may be watching and the other inspecting the thing as if it ticks, as if it might explode. I don't know how the crow came by the egg, whether it took it from a nest, or another creature did and was either persuaded to relinquish it or just left it next to some dead stumps for the crow to find. The egg is forlorn; there is no hope for it despite the crow's edgy circumspection, and it's already a bit cracked. It has lost the rocking movement

of an irregular sphere and, despite its apparent weightlessness, it now looks ill-defined, like crash wreckage. Eggs are powerful magic, especially at the vernal equinox, when they are associated with fertility and the Teutonic goddess Oestre or in Christianity, with the resurrection of the god made flesh at Oestre's festival – Easter. I approach egg mysteries like the crow, with caution. It is hard to imagine any human culture not seeing some kind of symbolism in eggs; spring in the temperate world means rebirth, life emerging from chaos, fertility, the egg as the incubated world. Even though it is unwise to assume all cultures see the same things, those tied to seasonal changes share a sense of eggs holding the magic of hatching life. Sumerian graves of 3,000BCE, in the origins of urban culture between the Tigris and Euphrates rivers in what is now southern Iraq, had carved and painted ostrich eggs for the dead. There may be no direct line 5,000 years later to decorated Easter eggs, but it is surely art's way of bringing Nature into culture, and civilisation's acknowledgement of life after death. Eating them is the crow's way of imbuing itself with egg magic. The carrion crow would appear to be a counter-intuitive symbol of regeneration. However, like the fungal and microbial alchemy of rot and decay in the woods, death creates new life and the crow is a gatekeeper between the two. Without further hesitation the crow breaks and enters the egg with the delicate surgical instrument of its beak. It does not guzzle but pulls a globule of yolk and swallows it as if testing a drug, waiting for something mind-altering to happen. Maybe it does, maybe the egg brightens the blue iridescence of the crow's wing, makes the black of its eye glint brighter than the orbiting space station at night. The crow balances on the equal day, equal night, of the vernal equinox; it eats the vernal egg and takes off, as Ted Hughes wrote, 'Flying the black flag of himself'.

DUNNOCK, tree sparrow, *Prunella modularis*

'Tseep! Tseep!' The hedge sparrow will not break audio contact with the group or stray too far from the safety of the hedge. Hedge is home: a forest realm ribboning through a landscape beset by dangerous space; it provides for a kind of dwelling that supports a very particular society. This passerine is also called a dunnock, meaning quite literally 'little brown bird', an anonymous, blended-in, could-be-anything bird. This one is prospecting for beetles, spiders and ants, as damp, mild, weather brings out early creatures. Its pencil-sharp beak shows that it is not adapted to seeds but it will take them from bird feeders if there's nothing else. Drab and grey-headed is the usual description (as is mine), but there is a subtle vibrancy to its oak-polish-brown flecked plumage with darker encryptions, and its head, the colour of lichen on branches. There is something surprisingly rapid about the dunnock; it's like being in the presence of a little ticking bomb. Its movements are quick and edgy. Its song – when it gets going in the spring – is somewhere between wren and robin, faster but less shrill and more codified, a rapid fire of erotic pulses that happen as quickly as it takes for dunnocks to copulate. These birds are quick and their sex lives racy: there's polyandry, with females sharing several males, and polygyny, with males sharing a female, and between them all they work out a metropolis of territories in the hedge. 'Tseep!' The dunnock listens for others to give him confidence to continue foraging. His call is familiar from here to the Caucasus, and is also heard in New Zealand where the bird was introduced in the 19th century by people who missed the small, drab, but highly sexed birds of home, to the detriment of New Zealand's native avian fauna. The dunnock furtles around the hedgebank in the quiet before the storm, before both a downpour and the shenanigans of the breeding season. For now, it quivers and flicks, attached by an invisible fuse to the hedge and, as if full of fireworks, this hedge is a box of sparrows.

EPHEMEROPTERA, green drake or common mayfly,
Ephemera danica

A golden swarm of mayflies danced along the rays of the setting sun between the river and the sky. This had been a strangely hot, dry spring; the sky looked blue and stiff with its corners swept and its harsh, bright spaces vacant. There were dusty mutterings about withered crops, hungry stock and empty allotments; when a cloud came by I crossed my fingers hoping for rain. Life sought shadow and moved less until birdsong, hidden, sounded like whistling trees. On May Day, we went to see the River Severn at an all-time low just downstream from the Iron Bridge. As tyres screeched around the Wharfage car park, we dropped down the riverbank into a silent cloud of mayflies, glimmering with golden light above the water. By the time the sun set behind the cooling towers, the swarm had vanished, washed downriver. The next morning felt like change, and by afternoon a gang of 20 swifts were

screaming around the church tower – they had come back
from their travels. The swifts brought new weather and a soft,
scent-releasing rain. The suddenness in the sky was charged
with swashbuckling clouds and a rain of birds that had arrived
in time to chase the golden swarms and iridescent wings. These
things were not just loose ephemera but essential elements of
a seasonal shift which opened the sky to May.

FOX, red fox, *Vulpes vulpes*

From under a dark hedge, a fox skips into the field. He is
darker than the ginger Highland cattle that sit chewing on
the corners of an autumn morning. He is darker than the
shadows of softly shredding lime trees, which fall slant-wise
across the grass. He is darker even than the rumours about
him, muttered only yesterday by the man who keeps hens and
wishes him harm. Except for the white tip to his brush, which
he twitches like a lamp, he is a very dark fox in the brightest of
October light. He threads between shadows further from the
hedge to step abruptly into the open, then pauses. There are
people about, but nobody sees him, no dogs catch his scent

and bark for him. The man who keeps hens says this fox comes through my garden. Now, still and watchful in broad daylight, he really is pushing his luck. Perhaps it's the glorious sunshine and the intoxication of an autumn that ferments inside every breath, but there's a recklessness abroad. A buzzard crouches then squirts a white signature into a field of warm earth and the soft green twill of winter wheat as it takes off into the sky. Crisp and blue is the buzzard's cry that cuts into the open. Inevitably, the ravens are provoked by such a challenge, and fly over the treetops to attack. The male raven stays above the buzzard, swooping and diving down to throw the larger bird off track. The buzzard slows, the raven misjudges his dive, and in that instant finds itself in front of those talons and beak that could easily end his life. But the buzzard is unfazed, perhaps just enjoying the ritual battle, and the two disappear beyond the trees. Meanwhile, the fox shakes loose from his indolent pose and tracks across the field using long shadows for cover until, under ash and ivy, he becomes shadow himself and takes what luck he has left with him into the dark.

GRASSHOPPER, meadow grasshopper,
Chorthippus parallelus

A meadow grasshopper jumps from the unknown into the known world. She is flightless and clings to blades of grass – a green-on-green invisibility. She is a behavioural thermoregulator, she follows the sun; she is nomadic on the south-facing slope of Windmill Hill, moving to find the warmest spot to help maintain her preferred temperature range, the bottom end of which is much higher than what she will find here today. It is cool and windy on the hill – nothing like the summer of a couple of weeks ago when the grasshopper song-and-dance act was electrified by fierce sunshine. She laid her eggs in one of the ancient ant tumps and hangs on in the sheltered thatch of the meadow grass as the wind stiffens, clouds thicken and the temperature drops. Maybe this is just a lull as weather fronts sail through and it will be sunny again tomorrow. Common blue butterflies find late greater knapweed flowers. Snappy little small heath and almost threadbare meadow brown butterflies struggle against the wind. The most rapid flyers are the silver Y moths restlessly testing their wings around the meadow before attempting the reverse migration south to North Africa when the swallows leave. The meadow grasshopper came here long ago and, at one jump at a time, she's not going far. However, she shares a common ancestor with a grasshopper in the Balkans and her genes tell a story of the expansion and contraction of her population across Europe along the edge of ice ages. She has an ancient lineage, stretching back 300 million years to the Carboniferous period when insects ruled the world, and before the meadow wildflowers and grasses she eats here evolved. A crow paces, darkly proprietorial, along the paths dog walkers, kite fliers and grazing ponies take, searching for such a resigned grasshopper. She flexes her hind-leg muscles, bends her knees so the cuticle clicks into a spring, then relaxes the muscles, releasing the energy that catapults her into the air. Into the unknown.

HORSE, Welsh hill pony, *Equus ferus caballus*

Two white ponies were grazing on the high slopes above Carding Mill Valley on the Long Mynd of south Shropshire. A mare and colt, white in the soft light that felt more autumnal than was usual for the turn, grazed on a hidden lawn surrounded by bracken and heather. Up there, they seemed still, absorbed in feeding, but whenever a dog barked in the distance, they became watchful. A pair of ravens flew across the valley and landed nearby. The ravens watched the ponies; the

ponies watched the ravens. When the birds flew off, the ponies
shook themselves from their grazing reverie. They seemed
to become present in the landscape, actors in the moment,
no longer passive. There was a strength about them; rough,
stocky and yet elegant with a sense of purpose as they stepped
across the steep hillside and shook their manes. This felt like
a declaration. There have been ponies on the Long Mynd since
Bodbury Ring Hillfort on the opposite side of the valley was
occupied in the Iron Age. The Welsh pony, from which these
may come, existed before 1600BCE and came from prehistoric
Celtic ponies that were semi-feral. My understanding is that
the true Long Mynd breed was one of the earliest in Britain
but is now extinct, and the present horses are descended from
Welsh mountain ponies, often described as pit ponies, used in
local industries for centuries. The Long Mynd is high heath;
the heather was still a vivid purple, the ravens called back
to a time long ago and the ponies walked in a place apart,
an island in a changed world. Reading 'September' from
John Clare's *Shepherd's Calendar* is to become aware of how
unpeopled the working countryside has become at harvest
time. The 'rude groups' who toiled the valleys are gone, as

are the working horses; the 'Rush bosomed solitudes' are no longer disturbed by workers but visitors, the harvest songs of the fields are replaced by the distant '*wuwuwuwu*' of midnight combines beetling across the flatlands beyond the hills.

The first harvest reaped by robots controlled remotely was accomplished at Harper Adams University in Shropshire this year. The link between the people and the land has changed radically and this gives the presence of the Long Mynd ponies a mythic status. Their declaration of existence now has more to do with the future than the past.

ICHNEUMON WASPS, *Ichneumonidae*

I admit to a macabre fascination for ichneumons: they are creatures of infinite diversity of colour and pattern, hard to distinguish and with highly specialised ovipositors or egg-laying tubes that can also sting and look like animated hypodermic syringes – nightmares for needle-phobes. They are insects as beautiful drones with their own ghastly intelligence. Ichneumon's scientific name in Greek means 'one who follows footsteps', a stealthy tracker that belongs to, according to biologist and author Bernd Heinrich, whose father was a world authority on these insects, 'mysterious and exotic wasps that are parasitic connoisseurs'. Each ichneumon species preys on a particular species of butterfly or moth. The ovipositor is for laying ichneumon eggs into living prey and some are so powerful they can penetrate tree bark and wood to inject a caterpillar hiding inside. The victims are not killed but stunned and continue to survive and feed as the wasp larvae eat the caterpillar's living tissue from within first and their organs last. When the host finally dies, the larvae pupate in or on the corpse, then emerge as adults, first to mate, and then the females go tracking. It has been estimated these parasitic wasps are the most numerous flying insects in our gardens and

there are more of them than bees, moths or flies. There may
be hundreds of ichneumon species around us that only a few
dedicated entomologists could identify and certainly tens of
thousands of species worldwide. We may know little about
them, but we can see their effect on fluctuations in butterfly
and moth populations. The holly blue butterfly community,
whose lifecycle switches between holly and ivy foodplants in
my garden, may be interrupted by the parasitic wasp *Apanteles*.
The large amber-coloured ichneumon, *Ophion luteus*, that
parasitises the great soft sofas of hawkmoth caterpillars, is
capable of stinging a human but they are not interested in
mammals; we should be grateful for their connoisseurship.
Parasitism is emotively difficult for those who empathise with
the victim, especially with butterflies and moths: the idea
that something so innocent and vulnerable never achieves its
potential for beauty but instead becomes an undead victim
of extreme vampirism, is a fear exploited by horror and sci-fi
genres of fiction. Ichneumons horrified Charles Darwin and
he saw in them an argument against the notion of the design
of a benevolent creator and wrote to his friend, the botanist
Joseph Hooker in 1856, 'What a book a devil's chaplain
might write on the... horribly cruel works of nature!' Richard
Dawkins characterised the 'devil's chaplain' as an atheist's
understanding of evolution as a blind process with no concern
for suffering, 'as an inherent consequence of natural selection'.
My own curiosity for ichneumons is partly to do with the way
our most bizarre, cruel and grotesquely violent fictions have
their origins, perhaps unconsciously, in the natural world, and
also to do with how the astonishingly beautiful complexity of
life has complete indifference to our thoughts and feelings.

JUNE BUG, May bug, cockchafer, *Melolontha melolontha*

The beetle stumbled giddily, as if it had spent the night banging against windows. A thumb-sized, bullet-shaped, grooved, blond-haired, conker-coloured beetle clung to a brick, soaking up warmth. It seemed heavy with the weight of its own folklore: chover, billywitch, bummler, doodlebug, mitchamador, midsomerdor, May bug, June bug. Its many local names around the country describe a character that swings between clown and pest; part rustic-comic, part economic threat, but now much reduced. The cockchafer may have received its most common name from a mixture of 'cock' as in familiar, such as 'cock-sparrow', and 'chafer' from 'cefer' or 'kaefer', a gnawing beetle, but there are ruder, rustic definitions. Having spent years as a fat, white, nut-headed grub munching roots in the darkness under lawns and fields, avoiding the beaks of rooks, the beetle on the brick emerged from its pupa at night. Like a toy car with transparent wings whirring out of open doors, the June bug blundered into the first light it detected. There's something about the beetle's antennae, the golden-lobed combs on its head, that made me think of aerials to pick up signals from an extra-terrestrial transmission, as if it was being controlled by some remote power. If so the signal seemed pretty erratic. The June bug, for all its comic blundering, was summer's herald, but then summer can be a bit of a joke, too. Flaming June is often merely flaming wet and cold. Just then a burst of sunshine changed the seriousness of dour weather. Such 'solemn stillness' was broken, as the poet Thomas Gray wrote in his *Elegy Written in a Country Churchyard*, 'where the beetle wheels his droning flight'. The June bug picked up the signal and took to the air with a determined but secret purpose.

KNOPPER GALL WASP, *Andricus quercuscalicis*

The oak tree that holds up one end of my garden washing line may have been planted by a squirrel or a jay 30 years ago and no one who lived here has had the heart to cut it down. The oak is a link between the greenwood and the garden, it brings wild things close. It has strange fruit: little brown apples covered in horny, foliate protuberances grow where acorns should be. They formed in August when a tiny gall wasp, *Andricus quercuscalicis*, inoculated embryonic acorn buds with her eggs. The oak responded in an entirely specific way to this wasp by producing growths known as knopper galls, a German name for a type of helmet. These wasps were not seen in Britain until the 1960s, but there was a spike in the knopper population in 1979, and people worried that the iconic British oaks were in danger of no longer producing viable acorns. Although that was unfounded, and oaks continue to produce viable acorns, the knopper gall wasps appeared as a growing cohort of climate-change species that are spreading around the world into new areas because of climate warming and globalised trade in horticultural products. Knopper gall wasps have spread as far north as Scotland, they have joined the rich community of life that inhabits oaks, one a native and one not. The galls are communities themselves, too, containing microhabitants, such as inquilines, in this case, cynipid wasps that lay eggs in the gall where their larvae feed on the oak tissue, and parasitoids, chalcid and ichneumon wasps that inject their eggs into the gall wasp larvae to feed on them. The knopper galls go brown and drop like windfalls. The wasp larvae inside them pupate and the adults wriggle out of vents in the galls next spring. The emerging wasps, exclusively female, fly off to find a Turkey oak, *Quercus cerris*, an evergreen introduced into Britain in 1735, to lay their eggs in its male catkins and form little conical galls on them. Inside these, by a process called parthenogenesis where females give birth without fertilisation, there will begin a second, sexual generation of wasps that does contain both sexes. When these emerge as adults from their little galls on Turkey oak, they fly to lay their eggs in the native oak, *Quercus robur,* creating the wonderfully surreal knopper galls.

LINNET, *Acanthis cannabina*

A choir of birds flew over Clee Liberty in Shropshire. Their voices sharply urgent, excited; they were not singing individually but their collective calls amounted to a glassy silvering of stones. Once perched in a tree all facing north, 30 birds fell silent. Apart from a bounding flight and ardent voices, their distinguishing marks were dark streaks that fell across their bodies, echoing the shadows from great oaks in the valley below. These were female linnets, birds that Aristotle called Acanthis, after a woman in Greek mythology that was turned into a bird. Her father's starving horses attacked and ate her brother Anthus. Zeus turned the sisters into birds so that they would not starve, they could forever feed on seeds of the fields and moors: finch-faced sisters, *Acanthis* their scientific name. The tree they perched in grew at Nordy Bank, the Iron Age earthwork ring on a common called Clee Liberty on Brown Clee Hill. The linnets have an older tenure than Aristotle's stories under this blue but hazy sky. A skylark launching himself from the centre of the earthworks soon vanished from sight even though his exultation could be heard from the other side of the haze above. This gave the feeling of being surrounded by an opaque wall: an enclosure further enclosed. The linnets, once collected for singing in cages, did not stay quiet for long. On an agreed signal, all rose together from the young, bare oak tree growing on a more recent earthwork made from quarrying on the common more than a hundred years ago. In perfect synchronicity, the sisters bounded through the sky, their voices fresh as rain.

MOLE, *Talpa europaea*

Just as dusk was settling in the woods, a darker thing lay across the path – an underworlder. The mole was stiff and dead. For all its 12cm (4¾in) length, this was a heroic corpse. The great, clawed shovel-feet which could propel the mole at 4.8km/h (3mph) through underground tunnels 1.6km (1 mile) long, were turned up to the sky. The mouth, with its tiny needle teeth that could gobble 36kg (over 79lb) of earthworms a year, was gaping. The nose, that created the olfactory equivalent of radar to image its subterranean world much more accurately than its pinhead eyes or invisible ears, was bloody. The soil in that part of the woods had all the consistency of a brick, a clay harder than kiln-dried, and may have forced the mole above ground in a desperate scramble to find easier digging in the fields. Maybe it was snatched by a fox; they are said to find moles unpalatable and leave them. Bad luck. The soft, smoky blackness of its fur would not last the night. When William of Orange's horse tripped over a molehill in 1702, grateful Jacobites are said to have toasted the 'Little Gentleman in Velvet' and celebrated the memory of the exiled King James II, who had died the previous year. John Clare was saddened by the sight of enclosure fences where 'little mouldywharps hang sweeing to the wind'. I don't know if the name he uses is long for mole, or mole is short for mouldywharp, but the notions of mould meaning earth and dead moles being displayed as an advertisement for efficient land stewardship are still with us. My local newspaper recently published a photograph of two proud molecatchers with a heap of 86 dead moles they had trapped in one field in one night. One mole weighing 100g (3½oz) can shift 6kg (13¼lb) of soil in 20 minutes, apparently.

The excavations of tunnels, lateral galleries for worm hunting and subterranean chambers for nests produce huge amounts of spoil mounds that kill Kings, make farmers furious and gardeners go mad. I once worked for a nurseryman who was so incensed by a mole digging through his plastic liner he blasted it with a shotgun and blew a huge hole through his nursery. I have worked in historic gardens where lawns had to be protected from moles using gas, poison, traps, sonic transmitters and all manner of devices. Moles are one of the main reasons I gave up professional gardening that involved lawns; they won and I have the utmost respect for them. The dead mole on the woodland path then was a pause for thought on the prejudices we inflict on the natural world. Its body was framed by white field roses, defined by their wild commonness as hedge roses that were never quite accepted into the garden proper – outsiders. The scene was of briars enclosing the sleeping princess, Beauty as a mouldywharp.

NEWT, great crested newt, *Triturus cristatus*

I was lifting a flowerpot from a neglected corner of the garden when suddenly I saw an apparition. Violently exposed to a bright interlude between showers, a creature lay unmoving: a hand's span in length, tail coiled in a question mark, its skin dark, warty and glistening. The tips of its toes were almost luminous orange and its eyes heavy, unresponsive to the world it had been so rudely exposed to. Instead of fleeing, the creature remained meditative, enraptured or stoned. This was a great crested newt: a creature with powers strong enough to confound the ambitions of property developers; a political animal with devoted followers. We, in the United Kingdom of newts, have more of this particular species than anywhere in Europe and yet, in the last 50 years, they have suffered terribly from water pollution, their breeding ponds being filled in, their summer hunting grounds and winter hibernating sites built on, and by disease transmitted by other amphibians. At 16cm (6¼in) long, the great crested newt is a charismatic amphibian whose existence in the liminal space between earth and water is beguiling. Females are larger than males, but do not have the vivid orange-and-black spotted belly, or the dragon crest down the spine and a separate crest along the tail. They secrete poisons from skin warts so powerful it can affect humans (don't try eating them!). In spring, they return to their ponds and the males show off their swimming dance where they fly like dragons through the water to attract a mate, depositing a sperm capsule at the bottom of the pond which is picked up by females to fertilise the 300 eggs they each lay on water plants. They continue their pond life hunting tadpoles and shrimps until midsummer, when they leave the ponds as nocturnal hunters of worms and slugs, until the weather becomes cold enough to hibernate under stones or in compost heaps for winter. The newt I disturbed remained motionless while all about it was frenetic: worms wriggled into cracks between stones, ground beetles scuttled away and woodlice blundered like bumper cars at a funfair, the smallest of them even trying to hide underneath the newt. There, the creature concealed its

true identity. Viewed from above it was as dark as the shadows that had concealed it, but its undersides were already showing signs of the sunset flame colours of breeding condition. Here was the salamander of myth, the fire creature that so fascinated Aristotle, a quasi-supernatural animal that grew new limbs (as does its distant Mexican cousin the axolotl) and could regenerate itself from a kind of magic that dated back to its origins in the Jurassic era more than 160 million years ago. For now, the soon-to-be great crested newt, protected by British and European laws that make it an offence for me to even disturb it, regarded being in the world through eyes that see trichromatic colour and ultraviolet, short-sighted in air, longsighted in water; through its forelegs that detect low-frequency sound and smell-taste organs in its nose and the sides of its mouth as keen as a viper's tongue. And yet it remained still; as I carefully replaced the flowerpot, its gaze was enigmatic and filled perhaps with too much knowing.

OTTER, *Lutra lutra*

On Islay, an island of Scotland's Inner Hebrides, you have to be unlucky not to see an otter. Unlucky like me. I had been there two days and not seen one. I spent a night on cliffs near the Ardbeg Distillery hoping to see an otter that wildlife filmmakers had watched in crystal-clear water below the cliffs. I didn't see it at all but heard one, I think, out of sight below me. On the west coast of Scotland otters are not infrequent but as I discovered, being there and being seen are two different things. I once knew someone who spent a year surveying otters in Wales. From prints and scat, he knew how many there were but had never seen one. I was more likely to see one in a river culvert under the shopping centre in Kidderminster, Worcestershire. The otter has become an icon of British wildlife and its return speaks of profound

changes in attitudes to wild animals as well as improvements
in environmental quality. It has also become a very literary
animal. Henry Williamson's *Tarka the Otter* (1927) and
Gavin Maxwell's classic book *Ring of Bright Water* (1960)
have inspired later generations. 'In moments of peace', said
Maxwell, 'such as I experienced that day with Edal [Maxwell's
pet otter] there exists some unritual reunion with the rest of
creation without which the lives of many are trivial.' Maxwell
was in search of a Wordsworthian romanticism to connect the
human soul with wild Nature and found it in his relationships
with the otters he kept as pets. The consequences for the otters
were tragic but Maxwell belonged to a generation for whom
keeping wildlife was, if not appropriative, certainly paternal.
As a young woman, Frances Pitt, who wrote the first *How
to See Nature*, published *Moses My Otter: Being the Story of
Madame Moses the Otter, and Her Sister Aaron; of Thomas Romeo
Grievous Otter; and Their Friend Tiny the Terrier* (1927). She
kept otters on her Shropshire farm at a time when they could
be killed by gamekeepers on sight. Frances Pitt's feelings for
the countryside, its natural history and her understanding of
animal behaviour was shaped by this close connection with
the animals she lived with. In more recent times the idea of
the captive animal released into the wild, and the cultural
influence of wildlife documentary observing animals in
their natural environment, has helped the otter, and other
wild animals, return to the rivers they were persecuted or
poisoned from. During the 1960s and early '70s, agricultural
chemicals seeped into rivers with devastating consequences
for an otter population already weakened by years of hunting
and persecution for taking fish stocks from anglers. But since
then they have seen a reversal of fortune. The cessation of
violence against the largest of the mustelids – the family that
includes pine martens, polecats, badgers, stoats and weasels

– has passed to an introduced cousin, the mink. This switch in persecution, together with the removal of many harmful pesticides and efforts to clean up rivers, has brought about the otter's impressive return. But they are still mysterious, elusive, literary beasts. The poet Ted Hughes described one hunted otter: 'Four-legged yet water-gifted, to outfish fish;/ With webbed feet and long ruddering tail/And a round head like an old tomcat.'

In a remarkable meeting in Miriam Darlington's 2012 odyssey *Otter Country*, she is thigh-deep in the river when she sees, 'Its ears are larger than I expected, almost like a cats... the live current in both of us prickles... it comes a little closer, *huffs*, then melts bodily into the water surface, leaving the shadow of a ripple and nothing else.'

PETREL, storm petrel, Mother Carey's chickens,

Hydrobates pelagicus

On the stormy edges of our archipelago, fluttering like bats while dancing a hornpipe on the waves, are small dark birds with white rumps and white striped underwings. These are storm petrels, birds not much bigger than sparrows that belong to the Procellariiformes – the tube-noses, having olfactory bulbs on their beaks for an extraordinary sense of smell – a family that includes pelagic giants, the albatrosses. The storm petrels are wanderers too, following fishing boats for debris and picking tiny fish, squid and plankton from the sea, which they turn into an orange, oily elixir. They fly back to land under cover of darkness to their nests in Pictish ruins, tumbles of cliff scree or island burrows shared with puffins and rabbits, to regurgitate the elixir into the waiting gape of their one and only chick. At sea they are largely silent; in flight they chatter on the wind; in their holes males produce a chesty purring punctuated by a sharp sigh, a sound described by naturalist

Charles Oldham as, 'like a fairy being sick'. Using recordings
of this strange song, ornithologists are able to lure petrels to
be caught for ringing – attaching identification rings to their
legs – so that their epic journeys can be better understood.
In winter, the storm petrels fly south; some stay around the
Mediterranean, others venture to the coasts of Namibia and
South Africa. In their breeding colonies on land petrels are
very vulnerable and can no longer be found on islands with
rats and cats; they are also predated by skuas, black-backed
gulls, owls and falcons. Outside breeding time, the petrels are
truly pelagic, dwellers of wild oceans. Mariners were wary of
them and their almost supernatural ability to thrive in trouble
at sea. Their strange nocturnal song, their odd fluttering dance
over the water, and their appearance before a gale earned them
a reputation as harbingers of disaster, storm and shipwreck.
They were named 'Mother Carey's chickens' after the Mother
of storms and wife of the dreaded Davey Jones, whose locker
at the bottom of the sea awaited the drowned; a flock of them
were the souls of those who died at sea trying to find their
way back to land. However, the Russian poet Maxim Gorky,
in his 1901 poem, 'The Song of the Stormy Petrel' saw that
the storm the petrel announced was revolution and the bird
became the emblem of revolutionaries: 'Petrel proudly soaring
in the/lightening over the sea's roar of fury; cries of victory the
prophet:/let the tempest come strike harder!'

QUEEN BEE, buff-tailed bumblebee, large earth
bumblebee, *Bombus terrestris*

A couple up the road invited us round for coffee and said
they had something to show us. They pulled out a parasol
for their patio table that had been rolled up and stored in the
garage since last year as it been too wet and cold for them
to sit outside until now. On unfurling the parasol, they were

shocked to find strange creatures inside. What were they and were they alive or dead? Some of the folds in the fabric held rows of cells, each containing a single ghostly-white creature like an alien sarcophagus. This is the life's work of a queen bee, the buff-tailed or large earth bumblebee. Perhaps she was a solitary queen from a nest abandoned due to flooding. She was monandrous and mated with only one male before beginning a colony of her own. With the weather so wet and the ground waterlogged, she went in search of a new place, crawled under the garage door and found the long dark tunnels into the furled parasol very similar to abandoned rodent burrows she was searching for. British queens are large, black and furry, 18mm (¾in) long with a brown collar, an orange-brown band across the middle of the abdomen and a pale buff tail. She would stay in the parasol over winter and lay a small batch of diploid (fertilised) eggs in spring, feeding the larvae with nectar and pollen she gathered from gardens herself. They pupated to become workers, an all-female, non-breeding caste that are similar but 13mm (½in) long. The workers foraged in soggy gardens for nectar and pollen, learning to tell the difference between flower colours to find those with the richest stores of food. They fed this to the larvae of more eggs laid by the queen; how they fed individuals determined the amount of juvenile hormone biosynthesis they would develop and whether they would become future queens. Males are from haploid, unfertilised eggs. And then the sun came out. On the first day of bright sunny weather for a long time, the couple set out the patio table and chairs to enjoy their coffee outside. They took the parasol from the garage and opened it...

ROE DEER, *Capreolus capreolus*

The slightest of movements made me pause on the lane.
It took a few seconds before I could 'magic eye' the dark
muzzled face of a roe deer kid through the buttery yellow of
field maple leaves. It was a twitch of the kid's ear that had
given it away. The ears flicked independently, listening intently
but not seeing me. As I stood stock still, the roe kid strained
its nose into the air. Then, as if electrocuted, its whole body
registered my scent with a shudder. Even though it now knew
I was there, the kid remained rooted to the spot. Perhaps,
as deer stalkers will say, it knew I was no threat; had I been
creeping around with malicious intent, its sixth sense would
have picked it up. Then I caught sight of the doe's tailless,
pale-patched rear end. She had been so engrossed in a lush
patch of grass at the wood's edge that she hadn't noticed me.
Her kid would have been born in June and she would have
mated last autumn. At that moment, a car sped up the lane
and I had to move out of the way. My eyes were turned away
for only a second, but when I looked back it was as if doe and
kid had never been there. Roe deer are the most numerous
species of deer in Britain and some accounts estimate there
may be a million of them living across the country. Fossil
records show they have been here for millennia, even though
they were almost hunted to extinction in parts of England.
New plantations, old woods and natural regeneration in towns
and cities have been an advantage for them, but foresters
and conservationists are concerned about the damage to
vegetation from so much browsing, so deerstalking for sport
and population culling is practiced. As I left the space where
I'd seen the roe deer, a band of buzzards turned around
an invisible axis in a sky so thick with cloud there were no
shadows on the fields. I ducked into the wood where the deer
had vanished. It felt reassuring to be on their side of the hedge,

away from the lane's traffic and fields which had a slightly toxic feel to their scraped openness. Inside was darker, richer with an autumnal, beery scent of fallen leaves and green moss. A morning rain had loosened the melancholy of the wood in muted colours and smells, softening the soil. As I climbed up a steep bank, I heard for a split second the rushing pound of hooves on earth. Then I felt something brush against my back. I spun round to see a third deer, a young buck, dark-faced, russet flanked and thorn antlered, following another over the brink of the bank and away into darkness. According to Robert Graves in his seminal neopagan work, *The White Goddess*, the roebuck is a magical creature of ancient mythology and in Celtic culture is symbolised as the object of the hunt, hiding in a thicket of 22 sacred trees; it's symbolic meaning is 'Hiding the Secret'. Graves says the poet's question must be 'But where exactly is the beast lodged in the grove?' And I feel that in my own experience of a fleeting moment, the roe deer is asking me 'where' something is, the place of its existence; within this question lies the atavistic hunting instinct of how to see Nature.

SNAIL, brown-lipped snail, banded snail, *Cepaea nemoralis*

At first sight, the brown-lipped snails looked like buttons stitched on fence posts and nettle stems in a corner of the field. They appeared passive and inanimate, yet they were quietly doing what they've done for millions of years – adapting. The rain had brought them out. Although snails have adapted to dry land and to breathing air, they are still creatures of water. Much of their lives are spent conserving water and they spend 30 per cent of their energy producing slime, creating a mucus membrane that is hygroscopic – it attracts water, allows them to wear a wetsuit and helps them travel on a film of lubricant. Snail slime was once extracted from live animals and used in

the treatment of various diseases; it has antibacterial properties and contains allantoin, used in the treatment of damaged skin and elastine, a protein used in cosmetics for shiny smooth skin. Snails leave a residue of slime in the silvery pathways they have made on wood, bricks or concrete. When I see these snail trails, I am reminded of the artist Paul Klee's idea that 'drawing is taking a line for a walk'. I've seen some dotted trails recently that look as if the animal had been jumping or hopping; this is due to the snail's locomotion on a small part of the sole of its single foot to conserve moisture. The snail is a gastropod, a 'stomach-foot'. The brown-lipped snails have nutty humbug shells; no two are identical. Far from sedentary, they are as homing as pigeons: hefted to that particular corner of the field they may well have travelled a round trip at 1m (3¼ft) per hour in the past 24 hours, grazing on algae and decaying leaves, using sense organs to return to the same post or nettle from which they started. They are vulnerable to being eaten by thrushes, who smash snail shells on their anvil stones, as well as to hedgehogs, so their adventures are largely nocturnal. Snail travel inspired Alfred Watkins in his book on ley lines, *The Old Straight Track* (1925). Watkins saw ancient landscape features such a cairns, barrows, mounds and notches in hills linked by straight 'ley' lines that crossed the British landscape. Watkins speculated that ley lines were measured out by prehistoric surveyors holding two staves to sight a straight line across the landscape, a figure immortalised by being cut into a chalk hillside in Sussex, the Long Man of Wilmington. Watkins believed the ancient surveyor persisted in country folklore and place names connected with ley lines as the snail called the Dodman, 'The sight of a snail out for a walk one moist morning solved the problem. He carried on his head the dod-man's implements, the two sighting staves.' On the fence post, the snail drawing ley lines on its walk had now aestivated: withdrawn into its shell, sealed up behind a membrane that glued it to the spot, it becomes a walled-up anchorite, an ascetic, deep in meditation, connected to a past beyond even Watkins' imagination. The calcium for snail shells comes from lime in the soil and the rocks below, which 450 million years ago were formed from the bodies of their marine ancestors. Wenlock limestone was made from the coral reefs and sediments of a shallow sea, long before life headed landward. The fossils of corals, crinoids and molluscs persisted because such delicate, vulnerable animals evolved a way of drawing calcium from sea water to create a protective stone architecture. These structures are not only present under the fence post and nettle root, they are recycled into the body of the snail. And so it goes on: the drawing of lines, the circular shell, cycles of lives and molecules, and helixes of pattern and DNA, all the weathering of upheavals throughout aeons of history, concealed within a quiet, contemplative moment in the rain.

TURTLE DOVE, *Streptopelia turtur*

In the 14th century Geoffrey Chaucer described one of Britain's most enigmatic birds as, 'the wedded turtle dove with her heart true'. The turtle dove has long been a symbol of devoted love and its purring, 'turrr-turrr' sound (where its name comes from), is a cherished part of the countryside's summer soundtrack. Europe's only migrant dove, turtle doves arrive in April and return to Africa in September. They are smaller and lighter than other doves found in Britain, with cinnamon-coloured wing feathers, a plum-blush breast, greyish head and distinctive black neck patches with diagonal white stripes. Once common throughout lowland Britain, the population of turtle doves has crashed by 80 per cent since 1995. Changing farming practices, the loss of suitable habitat and food plants, shooting and trapping in Europe and North Africa when the birds are migrating, competing land-use pressures in their sub-Saharan Africa wintering grounds and climatic changes affecting food supply, mean turtle doves are facing extinction. Many people notice the silence, feel their absence on summer evenings. In wet, cold springs many birds only migrate as far as France and are unable to make it any further. Offspring born in France will go back there in future migrations, which means fewer will return to Britain. Farm conservation projects in southern England run seed trials providing ideal turtle-dove habitat. They prefer rough young woodland near areas of shorter grass and close to water. Field margins grow traditional fodder crop seeds, such as double turnip, as well newer types like oilseed rape and farmland weeds, such as fumitory, which turtle doves love. Wildflowers have also been in decline since the 1960s and the two are linked through changes in farming practices. But British agriculture cannot be blamed entirely for the loss of turtle doves; on migration, they are seen as a pest in North Africa and Mediterranean islands because flocks of them feed on crops, and 2–4 million turtle doves are shot every year. It may be a lack of education, or as in their wintering grounds in southern Africa, people see the problem as tiny compared with all the other wildlife issues they encounter. For many people in Britain, turtle doves are a litmus test for the countryside: if they go, what else will go too? Conservation projects such as the RSPB's Operation Turtle Dove are important because in many parts of Britain there are no more purring summer songs. In John Clare's poem, 'I Met my Love', he recalls, 'I met my love in Summer weather/And wandered down the lane/Like Turtle Doves we pair'd together/And shall do again.' Because these birds have for so long been symbols of peace, love, fidelity and patience, their loss is felt like our betrayal. The collective noun for turtle doves is a 'pitying'.

URCHIN, sea urchin, *Echinoidea*

The sea urchin shells, pinky purple, dotted 10cm (4in) globes, sold in seaside gift shops are all that remain of far more elaborate creatures; they're like trying to imagine a chicken by looking at an egg. There are hundreds of sea urchin species that exist from the intertidal shore to the abyssal plain 5,000m (16,400ft) down at the bottom of the sea. The shells are endoskeletons called tests, formed by the animal's ability to convert carbon dioxide in the sea water into calcium carbonate by using nickel to make an inner structure that supports the soft-bodied creatures. With hundreds of feeler-like tube feet using a hydraulic system to pump water in and out for locomotion on the seabed, they wander slowly feeding on seaweed, mussels, sponges and brittle stars, which they eat with a circular toothy mouth like a waste-disposal shredder, and for digging themselves into the sand. Sea urchins have protective spines that are dangerous if they penetrate human skin and are also responsible for their name. Sea urchin or sea hedgehog – urchin being a folk name for hedgehog – comes from the Norman French *herichon*, and was Anglicised as 'hurcheon', then 'urchin'. In the Middle Ages, before the name was applied to street children, an urchin was a mischief-making sprite or imp that could turn itself into a spiky ball. This shapeshifting has a fascinating parallel in the evolutionary ideas of scientist Donald Williamson (1922–2016), who proposed that early animals of very different origins hybridised to produce chimeras, a process he called hybridogenesis that was responsible for the Cambrian explosion of biological diversity 500 million years ago. To illustrate this, Williamson fertilised sea squirt eggs, Urochordata, sponge-like, filter-feeders, with sea urchin sperm – marine animals that did not share a common ancestor – to show that larvae could be produced from genetically distinct organisms. In hybridogenesis, half the genome of one parent moves into the larva and another part into the development of the adult, which is an explanation of why the larva and adult of many species that undergo metamorphosis are so different. Sea urchins are dioecious; males and females release sperm and eggs into the current which fertilise to create larvae that look like tiny glass easels. Williamson's ideas are very controversial, rebutted by some and supported by evolution scientist Lynn Margulis (1938–2011), who claimed objectors dismissed Williamson for not adhering to Darwinian orthodoxy. The roe within the test is a seafood delicacy in many parts of the world and the edible or common sea urchin is in danger of over collection and so may become farmed. Fossil sea urchin tests, called fairy hearts, snake eggs or shepherd's crowns, appear in English chalk deposits from the Cretaceous period and are said to have talismanic properties – perhaps the magic powers of urchins.

VOLE, European water vole, water rat, *Arvicola terrestris*

Valley Brook, formed from capillary ditches and streams in the fields of south-east Cheshire, is in spate from the February fill-dyke rain. It flows through a business park, parts of which

are a nature reserve, under the dual carriageway and through
a university campus towards the railway station at Crewe.
Once one of the most important rail hubs in the world, many
of Crewe's old sidings are becoming birch woods and the
stream somehow flows under this to join the River Weaver
towards Nantwich. From the footbridge across the brook
where it bends past an old, hollow-boled alder tree, I peer
into a little beach of grey sediment formed between the bridge
and the tree. There, stamped in the mud, is a pattern of stars.
As if to remind us that we, the mud and the water, all come
from a cosmic building site, the water vole has left its starry
footprints. The forefeet have four toes and the hind feet have
five with the first and the fifth almost at right angles. Early this
morning a water vole, about 20cm (7¾in) long, weighing 350g
(12⅓oz), rotund with chestnut fur that hides little ears and
with a tail two-thirds its length, hauled itself out of the brook
to sit on the mud and look around. This was dangerous; any of
the tawny owls, buzzards or cats from the housing estate out
hunting would want to eat a water vole. Their most notorious
predator is the American mink, *Neovison vison*. Prisoners of
the Hollywood glamour of their own fur, mink are kept in fur
farms, unless they escape or are liberated by activists. Since the
1970s, mink have taken to the waterways hunting fish, frogs,
birds and crayfish, and are partly responsible for the crash
in the water vole population. When under attack, water voles
'plop' into the water and stir up a smokescreen of sediment to
hide themselves, but this doesn't fool mink. By far the most
dangerous species to water voles however, is the one that lives
in the Wide World, 'that's something that doesn't matter, either
to you or me,' Ratty warns his friend Mole, 'I've never been
there, and I'm never going, nor you either, if you've got any
sense at all.' Ratty, so-named because water voles were once
called water rats, in Kenneth Grahame's *Wind in the Willows*

(1908), is right to be fearful of the world of people beyond the wood; they have polluted rivers, damaged habitats and introduced mink. Despite establishing Ratty the water vole as one of the most endearing wildlife characters for generations of English readers, within 100 years of the publication of Grahame's book, the water vole population declined by 90 per cent. Anthropomorphism is no protection. In a direct line from the footprints under the bridge to the bend of the opposite bank, there is a small hole just above water level. Water vole burrows run many metres from the water's edge so they can retreat further uphill and inland during floods and often link with hedges. Engineering works, ploughing, changes in land-use management and dense tree growth on riverbanks, make life hard for water voles. They are truly amphibious, needing slow-moving or still waters edged with grasses, sedges and rushes to feed on. They make meticulous reaping patterns with their incisors on grass stems, sometimes creating rafts from vegetation, which they also use for their ball-shaped nests and for bedding. The habitat quality, whether urban, rural or edgeland, is essential. In Estonia and Belarus, where there is good wetland habitat there are also European mink, American mink and a high population of water voles. Now on the edge of extinction in Britain, they have legal protection, and many river projects exist to reintroduce water voles, improve habitat and purge mink. Water voles were reintroduced to Valley Brook some years ago by the Cheshire Wildlife Trust. Actually, the most efficient control of mink will come from otters which, three times the size, will kill mink. In the meantime, the only defence for the defenceless are the stories we tell about them, and the public sentiment that they evoke. Even if we don't entirely believe in a reprieve for animals on the edge of extinction, it would be inhuman of us not to try to do something. Each species we knowingly march off the plank diminishes us; each species we extinguish through ignorance does the same; we have no excuses. Not knowing the future seems an argument for doing nothing; doing something, however daft or reckless, for other creatures gives some meaning to our own. When the Valley Brook is in spate again, I cross the bridge to check on water vole prints in the mud and, sure enough, there are some. Thrillingly there are also some otter prints. I just wonder what the otters are hunting ...

WREN, *Troglodytes troglodytes*

A wren looks from the hedge towards the winter solstice as if its tiny weight tips the balance this side of an axis between one year and the next. The bird peeps from its refuge of wren-shadow onto the prospect of open landscape: an old, agoraphobic geography steeped in omen and augury. According to R.I. Best's article 'Prognostications from the Raven to the Wren' (1916), in the divination game played by watching wren movement, who comes, who goes, and what messengers or lovers bring, the wren knows. Moss is stiff as

an old mattress with frost. Chaffinch and siskin blow from
hedge tops into fields of open soil routed by tines and tyres,
each rut and furrow running with water, so the rolling land
looks like a woodcut. The ooze and slop of mud seeps each
time the frost gives. Brooks are ardent, their songs stronger,
streambanks are scoured back under red root tassels of alder,
and streambeds are yellow-grey as if each pebble has been
picked out, wiped clean and put back. When it rained, cold
and hard, buzzards looked like glove puppets stuffed up trees.
Now a red kite lifts over treetops into a half blue, half grey sky
above a sheep pasture. Free from jackdaw mobs, the kite keeps
a slow tack, scanning for carrion. It barely moves its wings
but for a twitching balance like a tightrope walker's pole. The
wren is the Holly King, in folklore the king of the waning year,
usurped on the winter solstice by the Oak King, the robin,
king of the waxing year. The little bird shifts in its shadow and
whistles quietly for the hungry times at the end of its reign.
'We'll shoot the Cutty Wren, said John the Red Nose.' In this
old folksong, with savage irony, the wren is killed, butchered
with knives and forks and its spare ribs given to the poor. The
Cutty Wren song is said to come from the Peasants' Revolt of
1381 when the starving poor resorted to eating small birds:
the wren became symbolic of imagined revenge on a sacrificed
king. Restless cave-dwellers of hedge hole and mossy stone,
wrens will die. Despite their powerful presence, winter will
crush many of them. Although they're our most common
breeding bird, hundreds die every day from what we have done
to the world they live in. This one watches, a peppercorn eye
framed by a white stripe for far-seeing, second sight. Years
come and go, the wren knows. The thrum of its wings, the cock
of its tail, the voice now prayerful will turn into a conflagration,
'like a martyr on fire', as Ted Hughes said, if it survives long
enough to tip the solstice balance.

XESTOBIUM, death watch beetle, woodworm,
Xestobium rufovillosum

Tap... tap... tap. I'm typing on my keyboard late at night;
it's pitch black outside and with only a small desk lamp,
I am focused on the words appearing against the glow of my
screen. I become aware of another tapping that overtakes
my concentration; it is mildly annoying at first, then, like a
code I cannot decipher, it begins to feel ominous. What is it
and where is it coming from? Tap... tap... tap. I stand and
listen intently under the old roof beams overhead, trying to
find the source. When silence returns, I return to my work;
then, like a piece of grit, something drops onto the page of a
book open on my desk. It is a beetle. Now I have something
to worry about. 'In the night, O the night!/O the death watch
beating!' In 'Forlorn', the Victorian melodrama by Alfred
Lord Tennyson (1809–1892) the death watch beetle presides
over nocturnal anguish. The 'beating', knocking, ticking or
tapping at night is caused by the male of a cylindrical beetle
that has emerged from a 3mm (⅛in) diameter hole. It is
brown with a mottled sheen of hair that resembles the wood
it inhabits. The beetle creates the sound, which is surprisingly
loud for such a small insect, by banging its head, mostly the
leading edge of the thorax that protects the head, on timber to
attract a female. Perhaps the tapping is not simply functional
as a mating call; it appears to be like stridulating – the way
grasshoppers and crickets make a percussive sound by rubbing
body parts together, as do aquatic beetles and water boatmen.
Maybe they drum for similar reasons to woodpeckers and
other animals, including ourselves. However, this beetle has
long been associated with the church vigil when a body lies
overnight before burial – hence death watch, in the timber
frames of haunted houses and the collapse of once priceless
furniture. After mating the female beetle lays eggs in the

crevices of timber and the larvae burrow into it. 'Old oak is as hard as iron', I was informed by a carpenter replacing part of a 500-year-old oak beam in a house near to mine that was disintegrating because of woodworm. Hopefully, one tapping beetle does not make an infestation. Adult death watch beetles are active from May to July; they come into buildings from the trees they were made out of. Beetles that feed on dead wood are part of the arboreal community responsible for hollowing out the trunks of veteran trees so that they can withstand gales. They have the opposite effect on houses and they have burrowed into the heads of many writers alone at night, listening to the tap… tap… tap of time running out.

YELLOWHAMMER, *Emberiza citrinella*

She sits on the top branch facing the sun, warming the drop of Devil's blood folklore says she carries. The yellowhammers are excited, restless, playful. They fly, bands of buntings between the hedge, where they open themselves to the light for just a moment, and the field where they feed. Of all of them, she stays perching in a hedge tree the longest, lost in thought, composing what John Clare calls, in his poem 'The Yellowhammer's Nest', the pastoral spell that, come spring, will be scribbled on the shells of her eggs. At the tail end of winter, the bright sunlight is unfamiliar and harsh, but so welcome. After weeks in the swill of rain and mud a whole day of sunshine and blue skies is something to celebrate. The only presence in the huge blue vault of sky is the pearly glow of the waxing moon two-thirds full and the occasional silver bullet of a plane at the head of its vapour trail. The male yellowhammers in this sunlight are as citrine as their scientific name suggests; yellow as the crab apples stuck like gobstoppers in the tree's thicket of twigs. When the birds move together into the top of an oak they are bright as butterflies.

To me, the yellowhammer's song sounds like a shepherd whistling instructions to a sheepdog, but there is no proper singing to be ventured here yet, not the *'little-bit-of-bread-and-no-cheese'* or even the alleged Czech *'I-wish-you-were-dead-farmer'*, but a kind of conspiratorial muttering, excitable and bright. Yellowhammers, because they are so rooted to home hedges and fields over time, have accents. These speak a broad Shropshire winter-talk to each other as they have done for centuries. In recent years, however, gatherings like this have become uncommon and yellowhammers are at risk, particularly in Northern Ireland, and there are recovery projects to mend some of the damage done to agricultural landscapes to help yellowhammers and others. The hedge-top female is quiet. Although she doesn't have the flashy yellow of the male, her brown and chestnut markings make her as mysteriously encrypted as her eggs. She seems so still while the others of her community, perhaps 50 or so, are tearing around from hedge to field and back again every few minutes. I wonder what she thinks or sees. When I was a child I liked the British bird series of cards that were given away in packets of tea. For reasons I can't recall the yellowhammer was my favourite. I still like its name; its song, sound and flight; its manner of dwelling in the margins; the oddly un-British canary-ness of it; the *'little-bit-of-bread-and-no-cheese'* metonym my grandfather and father would recite from a nostalgically rural past. I found one dead on the roadside and remember distinctly the glowing beauty of the bird John Clare described in another poem 'The Yellowhammer' as, 'feathered wi' love and nature's good intents', every time I pass that spot.

ZOOPLANKTON

The wave smudges out something written in the wet sand of
Morfa Harlech in North Wales with a stick. I imagine it as
a spell cast to charm ashore those lost at sea. And so it does,
as tides ebb and flow, stranding the barrel jellyfish. These
extraordinary creatures, also known as dustbin-lid jellyfish
because of their size and shape, have been shipwrecked after
an epic voyage. *Rhizostoma pulmo* or *R. octopus* is the largest
jellyfish in British waters, it can grow to nearly 90cm (35½in)
in diameter and is harvested around Wales for high-value,
medical-grade collagen. Jellyfish are boneless, brainless and
heartless, and have drifted on ocean currents for 500 million
years, pulsing gently towards landfall with the same kind of
trusting faith as Dark Age-mystics who set themselves adrift
seeking divine grace. There are 50 or so washed up along
1.6km (1 mile) of beach; some are upside down, showing off
frilly, translucent pantaloons of tentacles; others are the right
way up, looking like in-vitro flowers on Victorian graves; others
are half-folded, resigned to this contortion without struggle.
Jellyfish are the largest of the zooplankton in the seas around
these islands, part of a life-swarm, mostly invisible, sometimes
luminous and essential to sustaining the oceans, they are a
floating world. *Planktos* is Greek for 'errant', meaning travelling
in search of adventure, a wanderer or drifter of the waters.
Holoplankton, such as jellyfish, spend their entire lifecycle
drifting on ocean currents. Meroplankton, may be the larvae
of fish such as eels, or shore creatures like barnacles, which are
suspended in the water column until they develop the ability
to swim purposefully and become nekton or attach themselves
to something. Imagine plankton as a library of books where
all the punctuation marks are present but there are no words.
Much of the zooplankton feed on each other or phytoplankton,
the photosynthesising, plant-like organisms, and this process

is essential for maintaining the carbon cycle and creating a carbon sink in the oceans. The barrel jellyfish feeds on smaller plankton, which it captures using stinging tentacles; its sting does not injure humans any more than nettles. Jellyfish are eaten by leatherback turtles and sunfish, while zooplankton is essential for basking sharks, fish and visiting whales. Beach walkers seem unimpressed with the jellyfish, repulsed even, as if these creatures are worse than the plastic flotsam and jetsam that litters the pristine beach. Out at sea, these plastics break down into tiny particles and are ingested by zooplankton. This is how microplastics and the chemicals they are made from are moving through food webs and appear in larger fish, such as salmon, and onwards into humans. Another definition of 'errant' is erring: deviating from an accepted standard, a kind of thoughtless drifting without heeding the consequences of actions that we are now, hopefully, aware of and beginning to tackle. In the meantime, the longshore drift of Cardigan Bay tumbles onto the expanse of Harlech Beach, bringing more barrel jellyfish: dreaming minds in a luminous trance, heading towards a hopelessly futile yet strangely inspirational end.

Bibliography

Aburrow, Y. (1994) *Auguries and Omens: The Magical Lore of Birds*, Capall Bann Publishing, Newbury.

Adams, W.M. (1996) *Future Nature: A Vision for Conservation*, Earthscan Publications, London.

Alexander, M. (2002) *A Companion to the Folklore, Myths & Customs of Britain*, Sutton Publishing.

Armitage, S. and Dee, T. (eds) (2009) *The Poetry of Birds*, Penguin Books, London.

Bate, J. (2003) *John Clare: A Biography*, Picador, London.

Birkhead, T. (2012) *Bird Sense: What it's Like to be a Bird*, Bloomsbury, London.

Blake, W. (1794), (2016) *Songs of Innocence & Songs of Experience*, Walton Street Press.

Bruun, B. (1975 reprint) *The Hamlyn Guide to Birds of Britain and Europe*, Hamlyn, London.

Campbell Palmer, R., Gow, D., et al, (2015) *The Eurasian Beaver,* Pelagic Press.

Clare, John. (2006) *Shepherd's Calendar*, Carcanet Press, Manchester.

Clark, M. (2017) *Badgers*, Whittet Books, Stanstead.

Cocker, M. (2014) *Claxton: Field Notes From a Small Planet*, Jonathan Cape, London.

Coles, G.M. (1996) *Mary Webb*, Seren, Bridgend.

Dawkins, R. (2003) *A Devil's Chaplain: Reflections on Hope, Lies, Science & Love*, Houghton Mifflin, Boston.

Darlington, M. (2012) *Otter Country: In Search of the Wild Otter*, Granta Books, London.

Davies, T.W. *et al.* (2012) 'Street lighting changes the composition of invertebrate communities'. The Royal Society *Biology Letters* (May 2012) DOI: 10.1098/rsbi.2012.0216

Davies, W. and Maud, R. (eds) (2000) *Dylan Thomas, Collected Poems 1934–1953*, Phoenix, London.

Davies, W.H. (1940) *Common Joys and Other Poems*, Faber & Faber, London.

Day, J. *et al.* (2015) 'Part-night lighting: implications for bat conservation', *Animal Conservation* (18 March 2015).

Eliot, T.S. (1940, 1991 reprint) *The Waste Land and other poems*, Faber & Faber, London.

Falk, S. (2015) *Field Guide to the Bees of Great Britain and Ireland,* Bloomsbury, London.

Farley, P. and Symmons Roberts, M. (2011) *Edgelands: Journeys into England's True Wilderness*, Jonathan Cape, London.

Forestry Commission, (2016) *Phytophthora – tree destroyers*. https://forestry.gov.uk/phytophthora

Foulsham, W. (pub.) (undated) *Culpeper's Complete Herbal: consisting of a comprehensive description of nearly all herbs with their medicinal properties and directions for compounding the medicines extracted from them*, W. Foulsham & Co. Ltd., London.

Gibbons, B. (1995) *Field Guide to Insects of Britain and Northern Europe*, The Crowood Press, Marlborough.

Globus, D. and Schubert, K. (eds) (2017) *About Bridget Riley: Selected Writings 1999–2016*, Ridinghouse, New York.

Gorky, M. (1955) *Maxim Gorky, Selected Short Stories*, Maxim Gorky Internet Archive (www.marxist.org) 2002.

Graves, R. (1975 reprint) *The White Goddess*, Faber & Faber, London.

Grieve, M. (1978 reprint) *A Modern Herbal*, Peregrine Books, Harmondsworth.

Griffin, D.R., (1984) *Animal Thinking*, Harvard University Press, Cambridge.

Grigson, G. (1980) *The Faber Book of Poems & Places*, Faber & Faber, London

Hadfield, M. (1985) *A History of British Gardening*, Penguin Books, London.

Hardin. G. (1968) 'The Tragedy of the Commons', *Science* Vol. 162, 13 Dec 1968. DOI: 10.1126/science.

Hart-Davis, D. (2002) *Fauna Britannica: The Practical Guide to Wild & Domestic Creatures of Britain*, Weidenfeld & Nicolson, London.

Heinrich, B. (2007) *The Snoring Bird: My Family's Journey Through a Century of Biology*, HarperCollins, New York.

Henderson, C. (2013) *The Book of Barely Imagined Things*, Granta Books, London.

Hollingdale, R.J. (trans.) (1995 reprint) *Friedrich Nietzsche: Human, All Too Human, A book for Free Spirits*, Cambridge University Press, Cambridge.

Hoskins, W.G. (1985 reprint) *The Making of the English Landscape*, Penguin Books, London.

Hughes, T. (1974 reprint) *Crow: From the Life and Songs of the Crow*, Faber & Faber, London.

Hughes, T. (1997) *Tales from Ovid*, Faber & Faber, London.

Jackson, K.H. (1971 reprint) *A Celtic Miscellany: Translations from the Celtic Literature*, Penguin Books, Harmondsworth.

Kavanagh, P.J. (1990) *Ivor Gurney: Selected Poems*, Oxford University Press, Oxford.

Mabey, R. (1996) *Flora Britannica*, Sinclair-Stevenson, London.

Mabey, R., (2010) *Weeds: How Vagabond Plants Gatecrashed Civilisation and Changed the Way We Think About Nature*, Profile Books, London.

Mabey, R., (2010) *The Unofficial Countryside*, Little Toller Books, Dorset.

Macaulay, R. (1966) *Pleasure of Ruins*, Walker & Co., New York

Margulis, L. and Sagan, D. (2007) *Dazzle Gradually: Reflections on the Nature of Nature*, Chelsea Green Publishing, White River Junction.

Marren, P. and Mabey, R. (2010) *Bugs Britannia*, Chatto & Windus, London.

Metcalf, S. (ed.) (1996) *Hammer of the Gods: Selected Writings of Friedrich Nietzsche*, Creation Books, London.

Monbiot, G. (2013) *Feral: Searching for Enchantment on the Frontiers of Rewilding*, Allen Lane, London.

Muldoon, P. (ed.) (1998) *The Faber Book of Beasts*, Faber & Faber, London.

Nagel, T., (1974) Honderich, T. (ed.) (2005) 'What is it like to be a bat?'. *The Oxford Companion to Philosophy*, Oxford University Press, Oxford.

Ostrom, E. (2015) *Governing the Commons: The Evolution of Institutions for Collective Action*, Cambridge University Press, Cambridge.

Ovid, *Metamorphoses*, A.S. Kline's version, Bk XIV: 566–580.

Perrin, J. (2010) *West – A Journey Through the Landscapes of Loss*, Atlantic Books, London.

Perrin, J. (2015) *A William Condry Reader*, Gomer Press, Llandysul.

Pitt, F. (1920) *Wild Creatures of Garden & Hedgerow*, Dodd, Mead & Co., New York.

Pitt, F. (1922) *Woodland Creatures: Being Some Wild Life Studies*, George Allen & Unwin, London.

Pitt, F. (1934) *The Naturalist on the Prowl*, The Macmillan Company, New York.

Pitt, F. (1940) *How to See Nature*, Batsford, London.

Rackham, O. (1990 reprint) *The History of the Countryside*, J.M. Dent & Sons, London.

Rackham, O. (2010) *The Ash Tree*, Little Toller Books, Toller Fratrum.

Raverat, Gwen (1952) *Period Piece*, Faber & Faber, London.

Riley, A.M. (1991) *The Natural History of the Butterflies and Moths of Shropshire*, Swan Hill Press, Shrewsbury.

Robinson, E. and Summerfield, G., (eds) (1973 edition) *John Clare: The Shepherd's Calendar*, Oxford University Press, Oxford.

Rose, F. (1981) *The Wild Flower Key: British Isles–N. W. Europe with keys to plants not in flower*, Frederick Warne, Harmondsworth.

Scott, C. (trans.) (2011) *Charles Baudelaire, The Flowers of Evil.* Project Gutenberg. www.gutenberg.org/ebooks

Scoular, K. (1965) *Natural Magic: Studies in the Presentation of Nature in English Poetry from Spenser to Marvell*, Oxford University Press, Oxford.

Simms, C. (2015) *Hen Harrier Poems*, Shearsman Books, Bristol.

Shanor, K. and Kanwal, J. (2011) *Bats Sing, Mice Giggle: The Surprising Science of Animals' Inner Lives*, Icon Books, London.

Taplin, K. (ed.) (1989) *Tongues in Trees: Studies in Literature and Ecology*, Green Books, Hartland.

Taylor, P. (2005) *Beyond Conservation: A Wildland Strategy*, Routledge, London.

Taylor, P. (2011) *Rewilding: ECOS Writings and Conservation Values*, British Association of Nature Conservationists, Cullompton.

The State of Nature Report (2016) www.wildlifetrusts.org/stateofnature16

Thomas, K. (1983) *Man and the Natural World: Changing Attitudes in England 1500–1800*, Penguin Books, London.

Tucker, J. & P. (2017) *Beckwith's Birds of Nineteenth Century Shropshire, with notes on surrounding districts,* Holbrook Design, Oxford.

Vera, F.W.M. (ed.) (2000) *Grazing Ecology and Forest History*, CABI Publishing, Oxford.

Vesey-Fitzgerald, B. (1969) *The Vanishing Wild Life of Britain*, MacGibbon & Kee, London.

Wall, T. (2014) *The Singular Stiperstones: Landscape, Reminiscence, Literature and Wildlife*, Tom Wall, Lydbury North.

Watkins, A. (1970), (1994 reprint) *The Old Straight Track: Its Mounds, Beacons, Moats, Sites and Mark Stones*, Abacus, London.

Webb, M. (1934 impression) *The Golden Arrow*, Jonathan Cape, London.

Wernham, C.V. and Toms, M.P. *et al.* (2002) *The Migration Atlas: Movements of the Birds of Britain and Ireland*, T. & A.D. Poyser, London.

Wilson, E.O. (ed.) (1988) *Biodiversity,* National Academy Press, Washington DC.

Williamson, D.I. (2011) 'Larvae, Lophomores and Chimeras in Classification', Cell Development Biology (2013) dx.doi.org/10.4172/2168-9296.1000128

Index